College and Other Stepping Stones

A STUDY OF LEARNING EXPERIENCES THAT CONTRIBUTE TO EFFECTIVE PERFORMANCE IN EARLY AND LONG-RUN JOBS

by Ann Stouffer Bisconti
with the assistance of Jean G. Kessler

THE AUTHOR

Ann Stouffer Bisconti is a social scientist whose broad experience ranges from market research to studies of human resource development. In recent years, a main study interest has been the educational and career progress of college students, particularly the relationships between education and work. *College and Other Stepping Stones* is her latest work on this topic and is one of a dozen reports she has authored or coauthored for the CPC Foundation. Her numerous other publications include four books and more than two dozen monographs, articles, and other reports. Currently she is the director of the Washington office of the Higher Education Research Institute and vice president of the Human Resources Policy Corporation.

Preface

THE PROCESS of completing this study of productive college graduates was unusual. First, the research was carried out for my doctoral dissertation from Union Graduate School and was not supported by any outside funds; the massive data collection and extensive analyses had to be performed on a shoestring. Second, at the time the study began and throughout the data collection phase, I was living abroad. Obviously, I needed help. The published volume is proof that I got it.

The assistance of the College Placement Council was invaluable. In exchange for publication rights to the study for The CPC Foundation (the Council's research arm), the Council provided the liaison with employers that was essential for gaining their cooperation, and also funded and managed the mailing of questionnaires and the followup mailings to nonrespondents. The collected questionnaires were all shipped to me in Italy. Jean G. Kessler, then administrative coordinator of the College Placement Council, is recognized on the title page partly because she assumed responsibility for all the data collection and was extremely effective in marshalling a "field team" of 70 employer representatives. She is recognized also because of her helpful comments and insights throughout all phases of the study, from questionnaire design through completion of the final manuscript which she edited skillfully.

I am deeply indebted to the employer representatives, whose personal contributions to these data collection efforts made the study possible, as well as to the 524 men and women who took the time to give thoughtful responses to the lengthy questionnaire. I hope that they will find some reward for their effort in this report of study findings.

The analysis of data from the survey was a monumental task because of the large number of open-ended questions, and I am grateful for the able assistance of Irmhilt Hamza and Alex Hamza in coding the questionnaires. Ida S. Green deserves special thanks for her excellent typing and for making it possible to keep the project on schedule.

Being without financial support, I was fortunate to benefit from free services offered by friends and family. I am especially grateful to Richard S. Nunn, director of research at the American Society of Allied Health Professions, who performed all the computer programming without charge. It is usual for authors to thank their families for their support and patience; in this case, the contribution was substantive as well. My husband, Raffaele Bisconti, and my daughters, Alessandra Ilus and Giulia Rachel, all spent many hours immersed in piles of questionnaires—coding, sorting, and turning pages. My husband also typed early drafts of the manuscripts and offered helpful suggestions on the content.

Finally, I wish to thank my doctoral study advisors. Alma G. Vasquez, as faculty advisor from Union Graduate School, provided effective guidance. Engin I. Holmstrom, then study director of the National Commission on Allied Health Education, worked closely with me on the preparation of the manuscript and raised important questions which improved the quality of the work. Helen S. Astin, professor of higher education at UCLA, deserves my thanks not only for her role as advisor but also for the many years of mentoring. It was because of her persistent encouragement that I finally decided to make the investment in study for the doctorate.

Ann Stouffer Bisconti

Washington, DC
January 1980

Contents

List of Tables

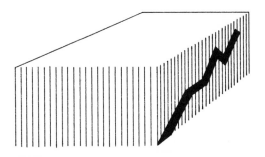

CHAPTER 1 **The WHY and HOW of the Contributions of College Education to Job Performance**

ALL SOCIETY depends on successful development and utilization of human resources for the maintenance and improvement of the standard of living and the quality of life. Employers require productive workers for maximizing profit. Individuals aspire to self-actualization partly through work. Wave upon wave of college students indicate that their life goals include not only financial success but also accomplishment in their field (e.g., Astin et al., 1974, 1975).

College education, traditionally, has been an important training ground for the professions and for management. Since World War II, the rapid growth of technology has emphasized the role of colleges in our society. Many different groups have a stake in the contribution of college education to job performance.

Nonetheless, parents who read reports of college graduates working as gas station attendants or janitors may wonder whether the financial sacrifices to send their children to college are worthwhile. The whole educational system, being held accountable for whatever seems to be wrong in the education-work relationship, is under tremendous pressure to change, and this climate creates special problems for personnel involved in curriculum planning and student counseling.

Knowing that graduates have faced a difficult and sometimes unsuccessful job search is important. In many instances, however, it is not very helpful for making decisions regarding ways of preparing current

1

and future students for the world of work. Looking beyond employment statistics to the process of competency development may be more useful in solving problems relating to the contributions of education to job performance. Likewise, efforts to understand *how* and *why* college education may contribute to effective performance on the job may be more helpful in the long run than attempting to place a dollar value on college education.

These considerations guided the present study, which draws upon the personal accounts of 524 college graduates. The objective was to place college education in the context of other learning experiences that occurred both before and after the college years. The histories of these men and women, who were identified by their employers on the basis of their "very good or excellent job performance," illustrate patterns of development that led to successful work outcomes. By comparing two groups—graduates of the mid-Sixties and mid-Seventies—the study shows how various life experiences may contribute differently to different stages in a career.

This investigation was conceived initially to address a series of unanswered questions raised by an earlier study that represented a first step in the exploration of how educational content is used in work. This previous study was carried out by the Higher Education Research Institute in Los Angeles for the National Institute of Education and The CPC Foundation and resulted in three publications (Bisconti and Solmon, 1976 and 1977; Solmon et al., 1977). A large majority of respondents to this national survey reported that their college education was at least somewhat useful for their current jobs, and most used their education to some degree in their work.

Nevertheless, large numbers of graduates, even from the more obviously vocationally-oriented fields, acquired many of their specific work skills after college. In contradiction to the widespread belief that liberal arts courses are vocationally useless, the study found that fields such as English and psychology are considered valuable for many kinds of jobs. In fact, large numbers of respondents across occupational categories included English and psychology among the courses they recommended to students now preparing for jobs like theirs.

However, the study raised as many questions as it answered. If college education did not prepare people for all their work functions, how were these other skills acquired? Was the learning of skills on the job, as opposed to in college, a deterrent to performance? Was there anything in the college experience that facilitated on-the-job learning? How did work requirements and the use of college-learned skills change as these individuals advanced in their careers? Why did persons employed in various fields recommend English, psychology, and other courses? Specifically how is the content of these fields put to use in various types of work?

How the Data Were Collected

There are many possible reasons why a person may be an ineffective worker that have nothing to do with the competencies the worker brings to the job. The individual may be constrained from using competencies acquired in college and elsewhere because of labor market conditions, work environment, and personal problems. Instead of studying a broad sample of graduates and attempting to account for such constraining factors, it was decided to start out with a group whose work satisfied their employers and find out how they acquired the competencies that enabled them to achieve this satisfactory level of performance. In order to do so, it was necessary to initiate contact through employers.

The essential liaison to employers was provided by the College Placement Council (CPC) in 1977. CPC's assistance was solicited because of its unique contacts with employers and its long interest in building bridges between education and work. Employer representatives were selected from the CPC membership within the categories of private industry, government, and "other employment settings." These contact persons were asked to distribute questionnaires to 10 employees in their organization according to specified criteria:

- *Degree attainment:* a bachelor's and no higher degree. The study was planned as an exploration of contributions of undergraduate education to work. Persons with advanced degrees might have difficulty separating the benefits derived from baccalaureate and postbaccalaureate years.
- *Period of college graduation:* half in the mid-Sixties and half in the mid-Seventies. This criterion permitted examination of the contributions of various experiences to both early and long-run jobs. Comparisons could be made between (1) the current situations of two groups at different stages of development, and also (2) the current and early situations of the group of men and women who graduated in the mid-Sixties.
- *Level of performance:* "be considered productive workers (that is, their performance is very good or excellent; it is not necessary to attempt to determine if they are the 'best' workers)."

- *Evidence of achievement* (for graduates of the mid-Sixties only): at least one promotion since joining the company or agency.

Although type of occupation was not specified, representatives were asked to make an attempt to select respondents performing different types of work. Both the respondents and their employers were guaranteed complete confidentiality. Responses were returned in unidentified, sealed envelopes.

In all, 70 companies or agencies cooperated by selecting respondents, collecting sealed questionnaires, and returning the questionnaires to the College Placement Council. The total number of respondents from these companies and agencies was 524, including 256 graduates of the mid-Sixties and 268 graduates of the mid-Seventies.

Respondents were drawn from a wide variety of employment settings (*Table 1*). The private companies ranged from banks and insurance companies, to manufacturing and processing companies, to retail enterprises. Also represented, but to a lesser extent, were government agencies (mostly federal) and a few accounting, nonprofit, and research/consulting firms. About half the respondents were employed in the Northeast, with the remainder distributed in the Midwest, South, and West.

TABLE 1 ──

Employment Settings of Respondents

Type of Employer	Number of Companies/ Agencies
Accounting-Public	4
Banking, Finance, Insurance	8
Merchandising, Services	7
Aerospace, Electronics, Instruments	6
Automotive and Mechanical Equipment	3
Building Materials Manufacture, Construction	1
Chemicals, Drugs, Allied Products	8
Electrical Machinery and Equipment	1
Metals, Metal Products	3
Petroleum and Products (inc. Natural Gas)	7
Research/Consulting Organizations	5
Utilities-Public (inc. Transportation)	3
Government-Federal	6
Government-State and Local	2
Nonprofit and Educational Organizations	2
Other	4

Because most members of the College Placement Council are large companies or agencies which employ large numbers of college graduates annually, the study reflects work situations in employment settings of that type. Also because of the CPC membership characteristics, the study excludes persons employed in educational institutions. The net result is a heavy orientation of study findings towards career patterns associated with business and industry and the kinds of persons who become employed in such settings. Moreover, relative to the total population of college graduates, the sample overrepresents persons with engineering backgrounds. Consequently, where relevant, the findings are discussed separately for the various occupational groups.

Women, instead, are underrepresented, comprising only 15 percent of the sample of mid-Sixties graduates and 31 percent of the sample of mid-Seventies graduates. The higher proportion of women among the mid-Seventies group may be due to several factors. Recent women graduates have shown an increasing propensity for participation in the workforce and for careers in business. During the decade between the mid-Sixties and the mid-Seventies, the number of bachelor's degrees in business and commerce earned by men doubled, but the number earned by women increased even more, by 135 percent (U.S. Office of Education, 1976). Traditionally, teaching has been a more popular choice than business careers among women graduates. During the mid-Seventies, however, the job prospects for teachers were not promising, whereas a more favorable climate for women had developed in the private sector.

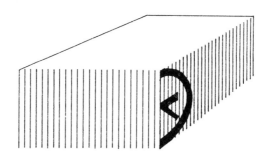

CHAPTER 2 **The Factor of Time**

MOST EFFORTS to assess relationships between college education and work are based on a static view of occupations which fails to account for the increases in responsibility and the expansion of job functions that may accrue to productive individuals over time. This static view results in a too-limited appreciation of the benefits of a college education. It focuses attention on the role of college education in developing competencies required for entry-level work, while ignoring the potentially valuable role in developing competencies that foster lifelong career growth and effectiveness.

One broad objective of a college education is to prepare students for work, and this objective may be accomplished in many ways. It may be done by teaching knowledge and skills that enable the performance of specific tasks and functions, by developing tools and thought processes that are of more general use in work, and by laying a foundation for continued learning. The payoff from the different aspects of preparation for work changes with time.

This chapter describes briefly the current jobs of the survey respondents and shows how the activities and responsibilities of the mid-Sixties graduates expanded over time. It then reports respondents' perceptions as to whether or not college education prepared them to perform these particular activities. In this instance, the focus is on preparation in the most specifically task-related sense. Subsequent chapters describe other ways in which college education and other life experiences built upon each other to contribute to respondents' ability to perform their jobs effectively.

THE TWO CLASSES AND THEIR JOBS

As a result of selecting both samples from the same companies, the jobs of the mid-Seventies graduates reflected fairly closely the early jobs of the mid-Sixties graduates, who, in the intervening decade, had advanced in their careers. The occupational titles held by the mid-Seventies graduates at the time of the survey were similar to those held by the mid-Sixties graduates on their first job after graduation (*Table 2*). Twenty-four percent of the mid-Seventies graduates were engineers, and so were 22 percent of the mid-Sixties graduates in their first job. At the time of the survey, only 13 percent of the mid-Sixties graduates still used "engineer" as their occupational title. Most of the others had become managers of research or technology activities.

However, the mid-Seventies graduates, as a group, had already progressed somewhat beyond "first-job" status. Few reported occupational titles classified as "other;" most of the titles in the "other" category are relatively low-level and likely to be temporary. Twenty-eight percent of the first jobs of mid-Sixties graduates are classified as other, but all of these individuals had moved over time into sales, personnel work, and general management.

When surveyed, over two-fifths of both classes were involved in science and technology occupations. Twenty-eight percent of the mid-Sixties graduates and 36 percent of the mid-Seventies graduates were engineers, scientists, or computer specialists; 17 percent and 6 percent, respectively, were managers. The remainder (over half) were engaged in business occupations and included management generalists, management specialists, personnel officers, accountants, and marketing and financial specialists. (A more detailed description of these occupational categories is shown in *Table 2*.)

Responsibilities increased, as a function of time on the job, in the four areas investigated: responsibility for work of a unit, supervision of others, responsibility for hiring, and involvement in decisions regarding company or agency policy (*Table 3*). For example, seven in 10 mid-Sixties graduates, compared with three in 10 mid-Seventies graduates were responsible for the work of a unit. When first employed by their present employer, less than one-fifth of both groups held this responsibility.

Accompanying these increases in responsibility over time were a variety of new functions. Of the 24 categories of work activities listed on *Table 4*, mathematical, scientific, and technical activities were performed by approximately the same proportion of respondents at various stages of their careers. To these mathematical, technical, and scientific activities, a list of administrative and communications-related functions were added over time.

When they first graduated from college, only 14 percent of the mid-Sixties group had administrative or managerial duties. A decade later, 72 percent performed these functions. Among the new administrative

TABLE 2

Occupations of Respondents

| | Graduates of Mid-Sixties | | | | Graduates of Mid-Seventies | |
| | Current Job | | First Job After Graduation | | Current Job | |
Occupation	Number[a]	Percent[b]	Number[a]	Percent[b]	Number[a]	Percent[b]
Science and Technology Occupations						
Engineer: Primarily engaged in engineering, technological production activities	33	13	53	22	65	24
Scientist: Primarily engaged in lab research	17	7	22	9	14	5
Computer specialist: Primarily engaged in data processing, system analysis	20	8	9	4	18	7
Research/technology manager: Supervises but not primarily engaged in research or technological activities	44	17	4	2	15	6
Business Occupations						
Office work: manager or analyst: Performs varied functions of overseeing office operations; performs policy and planning studies, statistical reports, industrial engineering, or contracting	30	12	25	10		

or supervisory functions performed by relatively large proportions of mid-Sixties graduates at the time of this study were program planning or budgeting (56 percent), personnel work/employee relations (51 percent), counseling (42 percent), and training (42 percent).

Increasingly, the work of these respondents required the preparation of written materials such as letters and reports. Two-thirds of the mid-Sixties group included writing as a current work activity, whereas fewer than one-third had done any writing as part of their first job after college. Increased responsibility also made it necessary for 42 percent of the mid-Sixties graduates to speak before groups or to lead group meetings, an activity that only 16 percent had performed on the first job.

The mid-Seventies graduates, after just two years on the job, provided

Personnel officer: Primarily engaged in personnel work, labor relations, industrial relations, or training	41	16	13	5	19	7
Accountant: Accountant, controller, or auditor	27	11	24	10	31	12
Marketing specialist: Primarily engaged in merchandising, selling, buying, marketing	27	11	12	5	30	11
Financial specialist: Insurance underwriter, banker, or investment broker engaged in financial analysis or evaluation	15	6	12	5	25	9
Other: Advertising specialist, artist, editor, teacher, social worker, secretary[c]	0	0	69	28	18	7
Total	256		243		268	

In this and subsequent tables:
[a] The number who answered a particular question may vary.
[b] Percentages may not add to 100 due to rounding.
The category "Other" has been omitted from subsequent tables classified by occupation because the occupations included are too diverse for analyses.

TABLE 3

Changes in Responsibility, by Number of Years with Company

(In percentages)

Responsibility	Graduates of Mid-Sixties				Graduates of Mid-Seventies		
	All Graduates (N = 256)	With Company 2–3 Years (N = 16)	With Company 4–7 Years (N = 34)	With Company 8 Years or More (N = 206)	All Graduates (N = 266)	With Company 1 Year or Less (N = 91)	With Company 2 Years or More (N = 175)
Responsibility for work of unit							
Current job only	51	19	35	56	13	5	17
Current and first job with company	19	56	26	15	17	20	16
Neither	30	25	38	29	70	75	67
Supervision of others							
Current job only	55	25	35	61	19	4	27
Current and first job with company	15	31	26	12	7	8	6
Neither	30	44	38	28	75	88	66
Involvement in decisions regarding company or agency policy							
Current job only	54	13	38	61	14	8	18
Current and first job with company	9	38	15	6	8	8	7
Neither	36	50	47	33	78	85	75
Responsibility for hiring							
Current job only	45	13	44	48	11	4	14
Current and first job with company	7	13	5	7	1	1	1
Neither	48	75	50	46	89	95	86

TABLE 4

Activities Performed on Job

(In percentages)

Activity	Graduates of Mid-Sixties		Graduates of Mid-Seventies
	Performed Now	Performed on First Job	Performed Now
Administration, management	72	14	40
Writing, editing	64	29	44
Program planning, budgeting	56	10	28
Personnel work, employee relations	51	15	29
Mathematical, actuarial, statistical, accounting	48	42	57
Counseling	42	14	15
Speaking to groups, leading group meetings	42	16	32
Training	42	18	30
Public relations	30	10	21
Research (non-laboratory)	29	9	21
Data processing, computer science	26	10	28
Engineering	24	25	30
Clerical	23	30	38
Teaching courses, school teaching	22	7	8
Production, quality control	19	11	22
Publications	19	9	10
Purchasing	19	5	18
Sales, marketing	17	10	16
Technological development	17	8	14
Advertising	12	5	10
Research (laboratory)	9	8	9
Art, design	7	8	10
Other	7	3	11
Health service	1	3	2

a midpoint in the expansion of the most generally performed activities after a decade of work. Among these recent graduates, 40 percent engaged in administrative activities, 44 percent had jobs that required some writing, and 28 percent were performing personnel and employee relations functions. However, this more recent group had larger percentages involved in data processing, engineering, and production work than the earlier group, either initially or 10 years later.

Changes in Particular Occupations

Among the mid-Sixties graduates, the broad patterns of incremental responsibility were observed across occupations, but with some variation. Compared with other respondents, relatively few scientists or computer specialists engaged in administrative activities (*Table 5*) or program planning (*Table 6*) at any stage in their career. Even among these groups, however, more were currently engaged in administration and planning than they were on their first job. Further, administration and program planning were not limited to office work occupations. These activities involved large proportions of the research/technology managers and engineers, as well as office managers and analysts, accountants, and marketing specialists.

TABLE 5 _____

Involvement in Administration/Management by Occupation

Occupation	Graduates of Mid-Sixties		Graduates of Mid-Seventies
	Percent Performing This Activity Now	Percent Who Performed This Activity on First Job	Percent Performing This Activity Now
Engineer	45	3	14
Scientist	24	12	7
Computer specialist	20	0	22
Research/technology manager	93	18	87
Office work: manager or analyst	94	22	76
Personnel officer	85	20	79
Accountant	93	4	39
Marketing specialist	78	22	53
Financial specialist	73	27	28

Communications activities—writing and speaking to groups—also were not associated exclusively with office work occupations (*Tables 7 and 8*). At least 30 percent of mid-Sixties graduates in every occupational category and over two-thirds of the research/technology managers reported current involvement in writing and speaking to groups. Among accountants, whose first jobs concentrated largely on numerical work, 81 percent now were required to write and 67 percent to speak to groups or lead meetings.

TABLE 6 ────────────────────────────────────

Involvement in Program Planning/Budgeting Activities, by Occupation

Occupation	Graduates of Mid-Sixties		Graduates of Mid-Seventies
	Percent Performing This Activity Now	Percent Who Performed This Activity on First Job	Percent Performing This Activity Now
Engineer	52	3	28
Scientist	18	0	7
Computer specialist	25	0	22
Research/technology manager	86	17	13
Office work: manager or analyst	69	28	55
Personnel Officer	46	2	26
Accountant	67	19	42
Marketing specialist	56	7	27
Financial specialist	40	13	16

TABLE 7 ────────────────────────────────────

Involvement in Writing/Editing Activities, by Occupation

Occupation	Graduates of Mid-Sixties		Graduates of Mid-Seventies
	Percent Performing This Activity Now	Percent Who Performed This Activity on First Job	Percent Performing This Activity Now
Engineer	38	28	43
Scientist	41	29	29
Computer specialist	40	5	22
Research/technology manager	71	43	27
Office work: manager or analyst	72	28	52
Personnel officer	78	34	68
Accountant	81	22	48
Marketing specialist	63	26	40
Financial specialist	53	20	52

TABLE 8 ───

Involvement in Speaking to Groups/Leading Meetings Activities, by Occupation

Occupation	Graduates of Mid-Sixties		Graduates of Mid-Seventies
	Percent Performing This Activity Now	Percent Who Performed This Activity on First Job	Percent Performing This Activity Now
Engineer	52	3	31
Scientist	35	6	29
Computer specialist	30	0	33
Research/technology manager	77	25	33
Office work: manager or analyst	60	19	33
Personnel officer	78	32	68
Accountant	67	4	13
Marketing specialist	59	22	50
Financial specialist	73	27	12

Increasing Range of Activities

The foregoing discussion stressed increases, rather than changes, in job functions because, in spite of the radical career shifts made by some respondents between the mid-Sixties and mid-Seventies, the majority of respondents were still performing the activities they performed on their first jobs and had simply widened their scope of work. The net result was an actual increase in the number of different types of activities performed.

On their first full-time job after college, graduates of the mid-Sixties performed an average of 3.2 of the 24 different kinds of activities listed on the questionnaire. A decade later, the average was more than doubled—6.9 (*Table 9*). Graduates of the mid-Seventies, after some work experience and, in some cases, a promotion, had reached an average of 5.5 different kinds of activities, about mid-way between the average for the first and current jobs of the earlier graduates.

Some occupations involved a wider range of the listed activities than others did. Research/technology managers and persons employed in various office work occupations reported relatively many different types of activities, compared with computer specialists, scientists, and engineers. The general pattern, however, was the same for all:

TABLE 9 ——

Average Number of Different Kinds of Activities[a] Performed on Job, by Occupation

| Occupation | Graduates of Mid-Sixties | | Graduates of Mid-Seventies |
	Current Job	First Job	Current Job
All occupations	6.9	3.2	5.5
Engineer	5.6	2.4	5.3
Scientist	5.4	2.8	3.6
Computer specialist	4.0	1.6	3.9
Research/technology manager	8.7	4.5	6.0
Office work: manager or analyst	7.8	3.5	6.6
Personnel officer	7.9	3.7	7.0
Accountant	7.6	2.0	4.1
Marketing specialist	8.0	3.7	7.4
Financial specialist	6.8	3.4	4.7

[a] Twenty-four different kinds of activities were listed. Table reads: On the average, engineers in the mid-Sixties group performed 5.6 of these 24 different kinds of activities on their current job.

- Widest range of activities—mid-Sixties graduates now;
- Narrowest range of activities—mid-Sixties graduates on their first job;
- In between—mid-Seventies graduates now.

College-Learned Competencies

This study incorporated a question asked of two national samples in an earlier study of mid-Sixties graduates (Bisconti and Solmon, 1976) and a concurrent study of mid-Seventies graduates (Ochsner and Solmon, 1979). The question listed the 24 activities shown in *Table 4* and asked respondents whether or not college education had prepared them to perform each activity. The results provide an overview of broad functions for which college education provided necessary competencies.

From this study and the others which included the same question, it is evident that the functions for which college education provided necessary competencies were broadly similar for the two classes of students who graduated a decade apart. Both were about equally prepared by their college education for many of the activities listed (*Table 10*).

However, substantially more of the recent graduates were prepared in data processing, personnel work, and speaking to groups. The first two activity areas are relative newcomers to the postsecondary education scene; therefore, the fact that so many more students among the recent graduates were prepared in these areas is not surprising. The greater perception of preparedness for speaking among the more recent graduates is not as easily explained, although it certainly is encouraging. Perhaps college education, with its greater emphasis on seminar courses and student participation in the classroom, is successfully building the self-confidence and competency of students for speaking to groups.

Relatively large proportions of those performing engineering, laboratory research, and mathematical, actuarial, or accounting work felt

TABLE 10

Preparation by College for Work Activities

(In percentages)

Activity[c]	Percent of All Respondents Who Were Prepared By College		Percent of Those Performing Activity Who Were Prepared By College	
	Graduates of Mid-Sixties	Graduates of Mid-Seventies	Graduates of Mid-Sixties	Graduates of Mid-Seventies
Advertising	8[a]	10	29[b]	42
Administration, management	31	36	37	53
Art, design	5	9	33	58
Clerical	17	12	52	27
Counseling	11	16	23	61
Data processing, computer science	16	41	39	78
Engineering	30	30	90	87
Mathematical, actuarial, statistical, accounting	54	68	77	86
Personnel work, employee relations	17	35	29	51
Production, quality control	10	14	24	32
Program planning, budgeting	12	18	18	36

that their college education had prepared them for these activities. All these activities were performed by persons in scientific, technological, and accounting jobs who would be expected to bring basic competencies in these areas to the first job.

Many of the activities that tended to be added to jobs as careers advanced, such as administration, counseling, and program planning or budgeting, were likely to be learned after college. The relatively few mid-Seventies graduates who did perform these activities included higher proportions who attributed their skills to college education than the relatively large number of mid-Sixties graduates. Obviously, a small group acquires the skills in college, but the majority learn on the job.

Writing is an exception to the more typical patterns. It is the com-

Publications	9	8	35	38
Purchasing	3	8	15	24
Research (laboratory)	18	21	68	77
Research (non-laboratory)	19	26	51	71
Sales, marketing	13	21	30	39
Speaking to groups, leading group meetings	17	36	20	63
Teaching courses, school teaching	16	16	29	39
Technological development	10	13	33	49
Training	11	12	10	26
Writing, editing	47	40	67	68

Table reads:

[a] 8 percent of 1965 graduates were prepared by college for advertising work.

[b] 29 percent of 1965 graduates who were engaged in advertising work learned to perform this activity in college.

[c] The category "Other" has been omitted because the activities included are too diverse for analysis; "Health Services" has been omitted because of insignificant numbers.

petency area developed by college that was most likely to be held in reserve and put to use in later jobs. Only 29 percent of mid-Sixties graduates were involved in writing on their first job after college, compared with 64 percent on their current job. Among the mid-Seventies group, 44 percent already were engaged in activities involving writing. Yet, among those currently involved in writing, two-thirds of both groups stated that they learned to perform this activity in college.

As they progressed in their careers, respondents in almost every occupation engaged in an increasing range of activities for which they were not prepared (*Table 11*). Only for personnel officers in the mid-Sixties group is no change apparent. They were less likely than other groups to be prepared by college for their activities in the first place. This group, largely comprising psychology majors, entered an occupational area that has become an integral part of top management in large corporations, and, in fact, the personnel officers among the more recently graduated respondents included proportionately more with a business administration background. (The college majors of respondents in the various occupational categories are shown in *Appendix Table A-1.*)

Aspects of College Study and Their Use

As job functions expand over time, the relationships between college education and work become less distinct and more difficult to identify. The aspects of learning that college graduates draw upon for their long-run work are different from those they draw upon for their first jobs. There is less reliance on the specific facts learned in a major field of study and more reliance on general concepts and processes, as well as on developmental experiences that occurred outside the classroom.

Respondents in the two classes were asked to rate five aspects of their college study on their importance for overall performance of their current job:

- Facts or content of study area in which you took the most college courses;
- General concepts of study area in which you took the most college courses;
- Methods or procedures of study area in which you took the most college courses;
- What you learned in college in general;
- The study experience (process of doing the study assignments).

TABLE 11 ───

Percent of Total Activities Performed for Which College Prepared Respondents, by Occupation

| Occupation | Graduates of Mid-Sixties | | Graduates of Mid-Seventies |
	Current Job	First Job	Current Job
All occupations	42	59	55
Engineer	45[a]	66[a]	63
Scientist	48	63	68
Computer specialist	36	59	57
Research/technology manager	35	58	44
Office work: manager or analyst	44	53	52
Personnel officer	52	50	65
Accountant	38	78	58
Marketing Specialist	39	64	44
Financial specialist	43	57	51

[a] Table reads: Engineers who graduated in the mid-Sixties were prepared by college for 66 percent of the different types of activities they performed on their first job and 45 percent of the different types of activities they performed on their current job. The questionnaire listed 24 different types of activities.

Although most respondents in both classes felt that all five aspects of college study contributed something to their current job performance, graduates of the mid-Seventies gave higher ratings than the earlier graduates to aspects of their major field (*Table 12*). Twenty-three percent of the recent graduates, compared with 14 percent of mid-Sixties graduates, felt that the facts of their primary study area contributed "very much." Further, 35 percent versus 20 percent, respectively, felt that the general concepts of their primary study area contributed "very much." There was less difference between the classes in their ratings of learning experiences in general.

Engineers, scientists, and accountants were more likely than others to hold jobs to which the contents or facts of the study area made a substantial contribution (*Table A-2*). Among the mid-Sixties graduates, those who were now technical managers and were involved in activities other than their field of concentration tended to rate the more general aspects of college study—general concepts, the process of completing the assignments—higher than specific facts learned.

TABLE 12

Contribution of Aspects of College Education to Overall Current Job Performance

(In percentages)

Aspect	Graduates of Mid-Sixties				Graduates of Mid-Seventies			
	Very Much	Moderate	Little	Not at All	Very Much	Moderate	Little	Not at All
Facts or content of primary study area	14	42	36	7	23	41	28	8
General concepts of primary study area	20	53	22	5	35	41	19	4
Methods or procedures of primary study area	21	43	30	6	31	40	22	8
General learning in college	12	60	26	2	17	52	26	5
The study experience (process of doing the study assignments)	27	45	24	4	30	42	19	9

Accountants also acquired new types of responsibilities over time but were more likely than technical managers to continue performing work closely related to the factual content of their major.   Therefore, although the ratings of the more recent accounting graduates were higher than those of accounting graduates of the mid-Sixties on all aspects of college study, both groups tended to consider the specific aspects more valuable than the general ones.

Computer specialists and personnel officers in the mid-Seventies group were more likely than those in the mid-Sixties group to have studied in a directly-related major, and, not surprisingly, were more likely to find direct links between specific aspects of their college study and their overall job performance.

First Job Versus Overall Career Development

Four of the aspects of college study form a continuum from most specific to most general:

Most Specific

- Facts or content of study area in which you took the most college courses;
- General concepts of study area in which you took the most college courses;
- What you learned in college in general;
- The study experience (process of doing the study assignments).

Most General

Graduates of the mid-Sixties were asked to select the one aspect that contributed most to their ability to perform their first full-time job after college and the one that contributed most to their overall career development.   "Facts or content of the primary study area" was selected by 29 percent for the first job and by only 8 percent for overall career development (*Table 13*).   There was little difference between the other three aspects but, clearly, the most specific aspect of college study yielded to more general aspects in its value for work as time passed.

TABLE 13 _____

Most Useful Aspect of College Education: Graduates of Mid-Sixties

(In percentages)

Aspect	For First Job	For Overall Career Development
Facts or content or primary study area	29	8
General concepts of primary study area	27	33
General learning in college	21	31
The study experience (process of doing the study assignments)	22	29

It seems that the different patterns of use of course content over time are most applicable to those whose major and occupation are closely linked traditionally. The comments of engineers, scientists, and accountants indicated that they viewed the facts of their field as prerequisites for entry. Those still involved primarily in technical activities tended to find the concepts of their field most valuable for career advancement, in that they helped develop new knowledge and skills in their field which were more relevant to current jobs or more sophisticated than the facts learned in college.

> **Design Engineer,** majored in engineering: "Engineering is a specialized discipline. A graduate usually works in narrow portions of his or her field of study. A supervisor, however, must utilize a wider base to make decisions which will stand the test of time."
>
> **Chemist,** majored in chemistry: "My job now requires considerable factual information about organic chemistry as it always has, but with less supervision than in my first job. I must use more abstract, more diffused, more general concepts to make decisions in research areas, where facts don't exist—yet!"

On the other hand, those engaged primarily in administrative activities tended to select aspects of college not necessarily related to their major—general knowledge acquired and the study experience in general—as most valuable for career advancement.

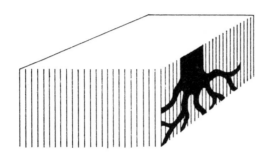

CHAPTER 3 **The Many Roots of Effective Job Performance**

TYPICALLY, the contribution of college education to work is assessed in isolation from other life experiences, as though no work-relevant learning took place either before or afterwards. Instead, the college years are but one phase of a continuous learning process. How important are the college years in relation to other life experiences for developing the ability to perform work competently? What are the types of work-related competencies to which college education contributes best? How does college education tie in with earlier and later life experiences in providing work competencies for continuing career development?

LEARNING SOURCES RATED

Respondents were asked to rate seven learning sources on the extent to which each contributed to the acquisition of the knowledge and skills required for performing their *primary* work activity. These work experiences included: course(s) in college major, other college course(s), college study in general, extracurricular activities while in college, work experience prior to graduating from college, company formal training program, general on-the-job experience.

For reference, the primary activities for which these experiences were rated and the distribution of respondents within these activities are shown in *Table 14.* They clearly reflect the greater involvement of the earlier graduates in administration; one-third of the mid-Sixties graduates checked administration, compared with 13 percent of the mid-Seventies graduates.

Verbatim comments showed that the frame of reference for answering questions regarding the primary activity was broad. Primary activity (e.g., administration, engineering, the personnel function, marketing) was conceptualized by many, perhaps most, respondents as comprising a variety of components: organizing, leading, speaking, writing, evaluating, meeting the public, solving disputes, hiring, firing, etc. Thus, when respondents were asked to rate the seven learning sources, they apparently reflected on the various tasks that were a frequent and necessary part of fulfilling their principal function.

The ratings (*Table 15*) show that the seven learning sources each made a significant contribution. There was a strong tendency, however, to rate the various aspects of college study as "moderately" important while rating on-the-job training "very" important.

College Experiences

Having seen how job responsibilities and requirements widened over time for the earlier graduates, it is not surprising that this group of respondents was somewhat less likely than recent graduates to give a high rating to the contribution of their college major. Nevertheless, 58 percent of mid-Sixties graduates, as well as 72 percent of mid-Seventies graduates, reported at least a moderate contribution of their major to the performance of their current primary work activity and only 9 percent of each group felt that it made no contribution at all.

Other college courses outside the major field and the college study experience in general also were thought to have some relevance to current job performance. Extracurricular activities are an often-overlooked learning source and, although rated lowest of the seven sources, did contribute, at least in a minor way, to the competencies of two-thirds of these graduates.

TABLE 14 —————————————————————————————————

Primary Work Activity of Respondents

(In percentages)

Activity	Graduates of Mid-Sixties	Graduates of Mid-Seventies
Advertising	0+	0+
Administration, management	34	13
Art, design	0+	0+
Clerical	0	6
Counseling	0+	0
Data processing, computer science	9	8
Engineering	11	16
Health service	1	0
Mathematical, actuarial, statistical, accounting	4	9
Personnel, employee relations	8	6
Production, quality control	3	5
Program planning, budgeting	4	5
Public relations	0	0+
Publications	0	0
Purchasing	3	3
Research (laboratory)	5	4
Research (non-laboratory)	3	5
Sales, marketing	6	8
Speaking to groups, leading group meetings	0	1
Teaching courses, school teaching	1	0+
Technological development	3	3
Training	2	2
Writing, editing	1	3
Other	1	3

Work Experiences

No matter how much college education contributed to the acquisition of job-related knowledge, a great deal still remained to be learned at work. The most highly rated learning source, by far, was on-the-job experience, which contributed "very much" to 9 out of 10 mid-Sixties graduates in enabling them to perform their primary work activity. Although mid-Seventies graduates had been employed after college for only a year or

TABLE 15

Contribution of Seven Learning Sources to Performance of Primary Work Activity

(In percentages)

Learning Source	Extent to Which Learning Source Contributed							
	Graduates of Mid-Sixties				Graduates of Mid-Seventies			
	Very Much	Moderate Extent	Little	Not at All	Very Much	Moderate Extent	Little	Not at All
Course(s) in college major	17	41	33	9	35	37	19	9
Other college course(s)	7	45	41	8	9	42	38	10
College study in general	17	56	25	2	17	56	23	4
Extracurricular activities while in college	6	28	36	30	12	21	35	32
Work experience prior to graduating from college	18	25	35	23	28	28	26	18
Company formal training program	24	35	24	18	30	26	17	27
General on-the-job experience	90	8	1	2	80	16	2	2

two, 8 out of 10 rated on-the-job experience as a very important contributor. Only two percent of both groups rated it not at all important.

Another source given high ratings was the formal company training program. Because these particular respondents were all employed in large companies or agencies, they may have had more opportunities than the average college graduate to participate in such a program. However, formal training programs were also an important source of job knowledge and skills for the respondents to the Bisconti and Solmon (1976) survey, who were employed in settings of all sizes.

Work experiences prior to graduation were thought to contribute very much or to a moderate extent to their current job performance by 43 percent of mid-Sixties graduates and 56 percent of recent graduates. Some respondents commented that early work experience was considered helpful, but the more related, the better. A sizable minority gave high ratings to the contribution of such jobs, even though they were held quite a few years ago.

Learning Sources and Occupational Variations

Of the seven learning sources, three showed considerable variation in importance according to the occupation of respondents and, therefore, are examined more closely by occupation in *Table 16*. The proportion who rated college majors as at least a moderately important learning source varied from close to 9 out of 10 engineers and scientists in both the mid-Sixties and mid-Seventies groups to less than half the financial specialists.

As might be expected, persons in occupations generally associated with entry from a specifically-related major field were most likely to acknowledge the contribution of their college major. Even for these individuals, however, the college major was almost never checked as the only important learning source. For example, among engineers, 41 percent of the mid-Sixties graduates and 33 percent of the mid-Seventies graduates felt that their participation in a formal company training program made at least a moderate contribution. Additionally, despite the obvious technical nature of engineering work, one-fourth of the earlier graduates and one-third of the more recent graduates checked extracurricular activities as a contributor to their primary work activity.

As was noted in Chapter 2, some technically-based occupations, such as research/technology manager and accountant, were associated with an expansion of workscope over time. The contribution of the college major to the *current* primary work in such occupations, therefore, was

TABLE 16

Contribution of Three Learning Sources to Performance of Primary Work Activity, by Current Occupation

(Percentages responding "Very Much" or "Moderate Extent")

Occupation	Graduates of Mid-Sixties			Graduates of Mid-Seventies		
	College Major	Extra-Curricular Activities	Formal Company Training Program	College Major	Extra-Curricular Activities	Formal Company Training Program
Engineer	85	24	41	86	35	33
Scientist	94	6	47	86	21	43
Computer specialist	27	11	75	89	17	67
Research/technology manager ..	53	43	59	60	26	80
Office work: manager or analyst ...	50	35	56	67	33	66
Personnel officer	54	39	62	84	53	63
Accountant	63	30	59	94	26	61
Marketing specialist	56	50	45	50	34	80
Financial specialist	46	53	74	36	44	72

rated higher by the recent graduates than by respondents who graduated in the mid-Sixties. The different requirements of early and long-run jobs in particular occupations may account also for part of the wide difference in the contribution of the college major to early and recent graduates employed as computer specialists. The principal reason, however, for this difference probably was the absence of computer science courses from the curriculum on most college campuses during the early Sixties.

Formal company training programs were a relatively important learning source for most occupations, but especially so for both groups of computer and financial specialists. This was the case also for the new marketing specialists, many of whom had a liberal arts background. However, for marketing specialists who graduated a decade earlier, the specifics of the formal training program were less dominant relative to other learning sources, such as the college major and extracurricular activities. Of all the occupations studied, engineers and scientists reported the lowest gain from formal company training programs.

In general, those who thought their work benefited greatly from extracurricular activities were employed in occupations that required management of people or a high degree of formal interpersonal interaction. Lowest ratings were given by scientists and computer specialists.

HISTORIES OF COMPETENCY DEVELOPMENT

In order to understand how the seven selected sources of job knowledge, as well as other learning experiences, may have contributed to productive work performance, respondents were asked to: "Describe in detail the history of how you developed the knowledge and skills required to perform your primary work activity. Starting from your childhood, if relevant, what (a) study, (b) work, and (c) other life experiences contributed to the development of your ability to perform this primary work activity?"

The histories were organized by asking these questions:

1. What experiences were mentioned?
2. What knowledge, skills, competencies, and attitudes were mentioned.
3. How do the particular experiences relate to the particular knowledge and skills?
4. What are the major themes regarding the developmental process?

Effect of Other Experiences

The histories provided a much broader perspective than can be gained from looking at the ratings of the seven selected "learning sources." Although these "learning sources" were frequently included in the discussion of how respondents developed their ability to perform their primary work activity, other experiences were mentioned as well (*Table 17*).

Fully two-thirds of both groups attributed aspects of their current work ability to college study. Other schooling also was mentioned, including pre-school studies and courses after college, such as night school and refresher courses.

TABLE 17 ──

Experiences Contributing to Ability to Perform Primary Work Activity

(In percentages)

Experience	Graduates of Mid-Sixties	Graduates of Mid-Seventies
Formal Education		
Schooling in general	18	21
Pre-college studies	18	26
College studies	64	64
Courses after college	18	11
Work Experience		
Pre-college work	17	18
Work during college	25	42
On-the-job training or experience	73	34
Other Activities		
Projects, hobbies	5	11
Scouting	3	3
Fraternity, sorority	3	4
Sports	7	4
Other school activities	9	9
Community activities	3	3
Professional activities, development . .	9	3
Travel	4	7
Military	8	4
Influences		
Parents	15	19
Siblings	1	2
Teacher(s)	5	3
Peer(s)	2	2
Religion	1	1
Personal problems and drive to overcome them	6	2

With respect to on-the-job learning, the mid-Sixties graduates typically spoke of postcollege experiences, whereas the mid-Seventies graduates spoke of experiences both during and after college. Given the short period of postcollege work experience of the mid-Seventies group, it is not surprising that employment during college was so dominant a part of their total on-the-job learning. The contributions of work while in elementary and high school also were described by respondents in both groups.

Current work ability was attributed to a wide range of influences that might not be readily associated with competency development. Many of these influences—parents, teachers, hobbies, scouting—made their impact during the growing years.

Important Competencies

> **Marketing Representative,** mid-Seventies graduate, studied economics: "As a marketing representative, the most important qualities or skills a person must possess in order to carry out his job responsibilities satisfactorily are self-discipline, time management, ability to work well with many different people, enthusiasm, ambition, ability to communicate, ability to analyze, understanding of what motivates people, and good basic common sense."

Table 18 shows the types of knowledge and skills, as well as personal qualities and attitudes, which respondents apparently considered important enough to mention as contributing to their work effectiveness. And, for the most part, there was surprising unanimity between the early and recent graduates.

Most salient—and most obviously related to job performance—were technical skills and procedures and knowledge of a field, followed by practical experience. In terms of total responses, however, there was a remarkable concentration on skills and abilities that are not occupation-specific:

- Interpersonal skills (ability to get along with, understand, influence, and sell one's self to others);
- Administrative skills (leadership, decision-making);
- Analytical, problem-solving abilities;
- Communications skills (speaking to individuals or groups, conveying ideas, persuading, writing reports and business letters, listening);
- And, to a lesser degree, numerical skills.

In addition, certain attitudes and personal qualities were considered important:

- Assertive qualities (self-confidence, drive, ambition; ability to work independently, to take initiative);
- Work habits (organization, discipline, neatness, promptness);
- Interest in the work;
- Work ethic (sense of responsibility, commitment to hard work, give the best you can);
- Moral qualities (honesty, tolerance).

Finally, some respondents mentioned the value of performing their primary activity of broad knowledge across fields or of working in a variety of situations and settings, and some referred to experiences that contributed judgment or maturity needed to make decisions or to carry out assignments independently.

TABLE 18 ───

Knowledge, Skills, and Attitudes Needed to Perform Primary Work Activity

(In percentages)

Knowledge, Skills, Attitudes	Graduates of Mid-Sixties	Graduates of Mid-Seventies
Technical skills and procedures	39	35
Knowledge of field	35	39
Practical experience, know-how	30	27
Interpersonal skills	24	27
Administrative skills	23	20
Assertive qualities	21	17
Analytical, problem-solving skills	16	15
Work habits, discipline	16	12
Interest in field or type of work	15	20
Work ethic, responsibility	12	5
Communications skills	12	10
Moral qualities	6	2
Broad knowledge	5	10
Numerical skills	3	6
Judgment, maturity	3	5

How Experiences Contributed to Competencies

What links did respondents make between their life experiences and the competencies which enabled them to perform their primary work activity?

Knowledge of Field, Technical Skills, and Practical Experience. Respondents attributed their acquisition of basic knowledge in a field, technical skills and procedures, and practical job knowledge to different learning experiences. Looking back, they believed that basic knowledge was developed from both formal education and on-the-job training and experience; technical skills from on-the-job experience and, to a lesser extent, college-year experiences, including work and special projects; and practical job knowledge almost exclusively from work.

A major theme was that college study is a base upon which technical skills are built. Persons in occupations closely linked with particular majors (e.g., engineering, accounting) tended to refer to such majors as contributors to the knowledge base. Those in other types of occupations were less likely to mention acquiring knowledge of their occupational field from the college experience, but some respondents did refer to college courses as a base of general knowledge which was necessary or helpful to continue learning on the job.

> **Engineer,** mid-Sixties graduate: "My studies at college gave me an engineering background and experiences, plus the ability to know where to go and find the answers to my questions. Through my experiences at work over the years I have continually expanded my engineering knowledge with day-to-day problem-solving plus the knowledge I have gained from courses offered by my company."

> **Accountant,** mid-Sixties graduate: "My profession is in a process of constant evolution where most learning comes from on-the-job training. Study (college) provided a broad conceptual framework of accounting which is in the background of all of current technical work activity with which I am involved."

Emphasis was placed by many on the need for a broad knowledge base to further continued learning, adaptability, and flexibility.

> **Chemist,** mid-Sixties graduate: "I am glad that I went to a liberal arts college and got a broad-based education. I have found that a good general chemistry education is all that is needed unless one works in a highly technical research field. The technology of most chemical industry R & D jobs is taught on-the-job and, with a job change every three years or so, a new technology must be learned. This is why a strong desire to continue learning is a necessity."

Respondents commented that career advancement and technological changes necessitate continued learning of the technical aspects of jobs, as well as upgrading of the knowledge base. Consequently, the earlier graduates were less inclined than the more recent ones to refer to college courses as their source of knowledge of their field (*Table 19*).

The importance of the workplace for providing technical skills and practical experience was explained, not as a weakness of college, but as a reflection of the dynamic quality of careers and the world of work. In fact, some respondents noted that their job duties were *too* specialized to have been taught in college.

> **Price Estimating Budget Officer,** mid-Seventies graduate, studied business: "My college background in finance and economics led me to my current job. My college background helped to round me out for my job; however, my specific duties are too specialized to have been taught to me in school."

Analytical Skills. In the development of analytical and problem-solving skills, college education made the most widespread impact on these respondents. College courses were mentioned by one-half the mid-Sixties graduates and three-fourths of the mid-Seventies graduates who described the development of study skills (*Table 19*). In fact, this competency area is one of the few in which the contribution of college courses apparently was greater, or more widespread, than that of non-college experiences. The ability to reason, to think clearly, to work through difficult new problems or design new techniques was often attributed to the requirements in college courses for discipline, logic, scientific inquiry, and creative thinking.

> **Associate Director, Insurance,** mid-Sixties graduate, studied business: "Education or study developed my ability to think clearly and to handle a variety of subjects simultaneously. Work experience was most important in teaching me responsible work habits and what to expect from employers."
>
> **Insurance Analyst,** mid-Seventies graduate: "Company training program was the primary means by which I became qualified for the job. The other primary training would be my liberal arts program in college (i.e., English major) which taught one how to think, not what to think. My current job involves analyzing situations, evaluating, and investigating."
>
> **Engineer,** mid-Seventies graduate: "The biggest asset, I believe, is obtained from learning the scientific method which is a method of approaching a problem, defining it, and reasoning it through in a logical, deductive manner."

TABLE 19

Development of Knowledge, Skills, and Attitudes

(In percentages)[a]

Knowledge, Skills, Attitudes	Experiences That Helped Develop Knowledge, Skills, Attitudes							
	Graduates of Mid-Sixties				Graduates of Mid-Seventies			
	Number Who Mentioned Skill/ Knowledge	College Courses	Other College Experiences	Noncollege Experiences	Number Who Mentioned Skill/ Knowledge	College Courses	Other College Experiences	Noncollege Experiences
Technical skills and procedures	84	8	32	88	85	26	33	69
Knowledge of field	80	39	42	59	93	62	26	36
Practical experience, know-how	69	1	9	96	64	3	8	94
Interpersonal skills	56	7	55	80	64	5	35	69
Administrative skills	53	8	40	85	48	15	42	56
Assertive qualities	47	6	41	70	40	10	33	68
Analytical, problem-solving skills	37	51	35	35	35	74	31	23
Work habits, discipline	37	11	43	67	28	11	36	54
Interest in field or type of work	34	9	27	89	47	13	23	87
Work ethic, responsibility	28	11	25	54	11	18	27	63
Communications skills	27	30	37	55	25	44	24	32

[a] Percentages are based on the number who mentioned a particular type of knowledge, skill, or attitude. It was not always possible to relate particular experiences mentioned to particular skills mentioned, so the sum of percentages for college courses, other college experiences, and noncollege experiences may be less than 100. The sum may also exceed this percentage due to mention of multiple experiences that contributed to the particular knowledge, skill or attitude.

Communications Skills. Another skill area to which college experiences were linked was communications. Sizable proportions of both groups of graduates cited college courses and other college experiences as aids in the development of their communications skills.

As will be discussed in subsequent chapters, communications skills were considered of high value to a wide variety of jobs and a factor indicating potential for career development. Many respondents, even in technically-oriented jobs, noted the importance of a good grasp of the English language and the ability to convey thoughts in an organized style in writing letters and reports. In addition, the ability to speak with ease was considered invaluable and, in some cases, attributed to college courses.

> **Personnel Specialist,** mid-Sixties graduate: "College gave a good foundation for writing and speaking . . . Overall, my basic personality and values developed at home with family; basic reasoning ability (not learned in college); writing, reading, speaking were developed in all schools; and primarily on-the-job training caused my professional development or achievement."

> **Management Trainee,** mid-Seventies graduate: "I believe that my management skills were developed most in my English and other communication-related courses . . . I would also suppose that the problem-solving mathematics and engineering courses which I took also contributed a great deal to my ability to recognize a problem, analyze it, and finally react to it (hopefully solving it)."

Interpersonal Skills. Like communications skills, interpersonal skills appear to have broad applicability to work. Many respondents, even in occupations traditionally associated with an orientation to things rather than people (e.g., scientific and technical fields), spoke of the necessity of getting along with and understanding people. These skills, according to some writers (e.g., Cross, 1976 a and b), receive much less emphasis in the school curriculum than they should. In fact, very few respondents cited college courses as a source of interpersonal skills. The primary sources were sports and extracurricular activities during and prior to the college years. Living arrangements—fraternities, sororities, and dormitories—also helped develop the ability to work closely and in cooperation with others. The ability to deal with people was then honed on the job, as a result of day-to-day interaction in a work situation.

> **Research Manager,** mid-Sixties graduate, studied chemistry: "Learning early the 'golden rule' and applying it to others. High school activities from student council and varsity sports to college

student council and varsity sports were a huge help in relating to others."

Systems Analyst, mid-Sixties graduate: "High school sports contributed giving me a feeling of confidence in myself, experience of discipline, performing in front of others, and cooperating and working together as a team. Working my way through college (due to financial necessity) gave meaning to my degree and taught me values and willingness to achieve. Selling life insurance gave me tremendous insight to other people and ability to meet and communicate with them. Learned how to meet complete strangers and build rapport with them and gain their confidence."

Administrative Skills. There are many components which make up administrative skills. In their comments, respondents focused on leadership and decision-making abilities. These abilities were rarely attributed to courses, an exception being courses taken by some business majors. Nonacademic college experiences did contribute, especially leadership positions on campus. Some respondents also cited earlier leadership experiences, such as scouting. For the most part, however, decision-making and practical aspects of management tended to be acquired with experience on the job.

Engineer, mid-Sixties graduate: "My experiences while being an officer in a fraternity—organizing budgets, programs, etc., and leading people."

Engineer, mid-Sixties graduate: "Job experience taught me how to accomplish my objectives through other people, to plan better, establish objectives, measure results."

Business Administration Specialist, mid-Seventies graduate: "As a child I was generally a 'leader of the pack.' I became an Eagle Scout on my 13th birthday and was selected first chair on my instrument in all-state concert band for all three years of high school. In the years following, I usually assumed some responsible role in my four-year military duties and subsequent jobs."

Attitudes and Habits. In many instances, respondents placed greater emphasis on attitudes and habits than on knowledge of a field. A recurring theme of the personal histories was the importance of discipline, interest, enthusiasm, willingness to work hard, and a sense of responsibility. These qualities were considered directly relevant to performance of the primary work activity and to continued learning on the job.

Respondents looked back to their childhood years, particularly parental influences, as sources of positive attitudes and good work habits.

Parents and early experiences—such as household chores, scouting, military duty, religion, and jobs—were described as sources of a strong belief in the work ethic and sense of responsibility. Some respondents also felt that these experiences instilled good study and/or work habits. Interest in the field also was encouraged by parents, as well as by toys and hobbies, high school or college courses, the influence of teachers or peers, and jobs held at different stages.

> **Assistant Biologist,** mid-Seventies graduate: "My study habits, work habits were also being bred into me as I grew up . . . The wanting to do everything right and accurately might have had something to do with the fact that my dad is somewhat of a perfectionist."

> **Research Manager,** mid-Sixties graduate, studied engineering: "I was raised on a ranch and was taught at an early age how to work. I know the value of hard work and have the discipline to work."

> **Engineer,** mid-Sixties graduate: "Working with my father during summer vacations helped me develop a sense of pride in overcoming obstacles and doing the job right. Part-time engineering work during the summer vacations between my soph-junior and junior-senior years at college allowed me to find out that I did enjoy engineering work and served to strengthen my desire to do well in college."

> **Personnel Manager,** mid-Sixties graduate: "It was my good fortune to have parents who instilled in me confidence, ambition, that good feeling that follows a job well done; accomplishment and peer respect and regard. Having a sound basic set of values with regard to others—respect for individuals.

Assertive Qualities. Self-confidence, ambition, and independence were considered important in carrying out the functions for which one was prepared. Of all the factors cited as necessary for performing the primary activity, these assertive qualities were least likely to be attributed to a single influential person, event, or experience; instead, they developed over a period of years. Extracurricular activities, especially sports, were described as sources of competitive spirit (tempered by a cooperative spirit) and self-confidence. A major influence, however, was experience on the job, which led over time to mastery of the job content and ease of interaction with others. To a much lesser extent, mastery of the subject matter in college courses also was mentioned in relation to the development of self-confidence.

> **Chemist,** mid-Sixties graduate: "Aggressiveness is also important along with self-confidence. These I have learned through my competitive sports in high school, college, and in being successful with the business world."

Applied R. & D. Manager, mid-Sixties graduate: "College and study formed a sound basis for developing the technical skills required to give me the confidence to do the management work I presently perform. Along with self-confidence and maturing came the ability to work with people to achieve pre-planned and organized objectives."

A Learning Timetable

Graduates of both the mid-Sixties and mid-Seventies traced the development of requisite knowledge, skills, and attitudes back to a wide variety of experiences that occurred at various points in their lives. These experiences were viewed as stepping stones in a continuous process of competency development. Some of the more common patterns are shown in *Figure 1*.

In the earliest years, basic attitudes and values were formed. Some respondents pointed out that no amount of technical skills could compensate for absence of these basic attitudes and values. Other foundations were interpersonal and communications skills and interests. Their development was not associated predominantly with any particular period and the range of influences was extremely broad.

Four types of competencies were most frequently associated with the college years and afterwards. College courses were the most salient source of analytical and problem-solving skills. A knowledge base in one's field, administrative skills, and technical skills and procedures were gained primarily from college on, although some respondents began to acquire them earlier. Overall, work seemed to play a more significant role than college in teaching technical skills and procedures, even among accountants and engineers, principally because skills and the knowledge base had to grow with the changing demands of the work. For this reason, the ability to continue learning was emphasized.

Finally, practical experience was attributed almost exclusively to work with one's current employer. Although earlier jobs contributed to practical experience of a more general nature, respondents seemed to feel that each new employment setting and each new work situation required a period of adaptation.

Although these broad patterns did emerge from the personal histories, the single most important implication of the findings is that there is no set way of developing knowledge, skills, and attitudes required for effective job performance. Both the range of time and range of experiences associated with their development were wide.

FIGURE 1

Developmental Periods of Knowledge, Skills, and Attitudes

Knowledge, Skills, Attitudes	Early Childhood	High School	Periods of Development — College	Postcollege
Practical experience				WORK
Technical skills, procedures		COURSES, WORK		
Knowledge base in field		COURSES, WORK		
Administrative skills			LEADERSHIP ACTIVITIES, WORK	
Analytical skills			COLLEGE COURSES	
Interpersonal, communications skills	BROAD SCHOOL EXPERIENCES, EXTRACURRICULAR ACTIVITIES, SPORTS, ENGLISH COURSES, WORK			
Interests	PARENTS, COURSES, TEACHERS, PEERS, HOBBIES, PROJECTS, WORK			
Attitudes, values	PARENTS, SCOUTING, RELIGION, EARLY JOBS			

CONTRIBUTIONS OF COLLEGE EXPERIENCES

The findings indicate that the impact of the college experience on work can be far-reaching. Most studies of education-work relationships focus on the college major. The experience of the college graduates studied here showed that the way the college major relates to work may vary, depending on the type of major, the type of work, and the stage of career development. The specifics of a field were most useful to respondents in occupations that generally require a particular college background for entry. However, as they advanced in their careers and became more involved in management, even persons in technical occupations began to draw from a broader knowledge base for effective performance. These findings are consistent with those of an earlier study that found an association between effectiveness in management and having competencies outside a specialty field (Huttner et al., 1959).

It seems that specifics may be useful or necessary for entry into and performance in the first job. Broader aspects of the major—the concepts and methodologies—appear to contribute as a foundation upon which on-the-job learning is built. They also appear to contribute directly to problem-solving throughout the work years.

Even when there was no obvious direct relationship between major and occupation, the major area sometimes contributed useful facts, concepts, or methodologies. Further, across occupations, the study process itself (just completing the assignments) aided job performance by instilling good work habits and responsibility, and college study in general enhanced communications skills.

Beyond study itself, many extracurricular college experiences were associated with effective job performance. Interaction with others, both in and out of class, was attributed with developing a variety of interests, new perspectives, and competencies.

Specific inquiry about the value of extracurricular activities and campus life showed that the college years were an eye-opening experience for many of these graduates, partly because of the contact with people. In general, meeting new people at college was credited with developing self-confidence and interpersonal skills, and for learning to get along with others.

Management Trainee, mid-Seventies graduate: "Meeting new people, having to associate with others under new and different circumstances contributed to my being able to get along with others."

Petroleum Supply Analyst, mid-Seventies graduate: "The experiences in meeting and dealing with people at college have been an invaluable source of reference for my job. I deal with new people every day. College taught me to be tolerant of their differences and to respect those differences. I have learned to listen."

Graduates in both groups described how the college experience contributed to their ability to perform their work through contact with persons from different social or ethnic backgrounds. Getting to know people from different races and social classes developed awareness of and tolerance for different values. It also increased respondents' ability to communicate with persons whose experiences and ideas might be different from their own.

Accountant, Managing Partner, mid-Sixties graduate: "Throughout college and subsequently, the opportunity to meet and deal with new people with diverse backgrounds contributes greatly to one's ability to understand people, become better listeners, and understand how important empathy is in dealing with people."

Engineer, mid-Sixties graduate: Dealing with people is an integral part of any job function. In my present job, I have to deal with individuals whose background and values are very different from my own. Encountering a wide range of people at college has enabled me to survive in the environment of my present job."

Life Insurance Analyst, mid-Seventies graduate: "The resident assistant position I held in college enabled me to meet people from various backgrounds and discuss many ideas pertaining not only to college life but life in general. Since I work with many different types of people from various backgrounds, this has helped me to make many friends very quickly in my office. I feel this is important since I must rely on many people to perform my job function effectively."

Others cited intellectual interaction or exchange of ideas that benefited their job performance. Brainstorming and working together with college faculty and peers in their field or in other fields helped to develop depth or breadth of knowledge and perspectives. In addition it helped to develop both career directions and self-confidence regarding one's verbal capabilities.

Manager, Product Safety, mid-Sixties graduate: "Learning from peers—trying to 'measure up' to those who were more successful and gaining a competitive spirit. Some of the best college professors I had taught students to think positively—develop a positive attitude toward self and goals—as much as they taught subject matter."

> **Marketing Manager,** mid-Sixties graduate: "The university experience was a chance for me to try out and strengthen some of the concepts I began to form late in high school and prep school. When I arrived at university I didn't know specifically what I wanted to do when I graduated. Therefore, the four years were a very important part of my life and all the people (professors, counselors, graduate students, students, coaches, etc.) had a great effect on shaping the way I think and act today."

> **Chemical Engineer,** mid-Seventies graduate: "One of the most valuable experiences of my college education was learning to communicate with people on an academic level."

Certain activities or arrangements facilitated intellectual and social interaction. Living in a fraternity, sorority, or dormitory was thought to develop interpersonal skills and to promote getting along with others and working towards a common goal.

> **Research Analyst,** mid-Seventies graduate: "The close proximity with many people in a dorm or fraternity provides a chance to learn a great deal about people. First time out of a family living situation."

> **Manager, Systems and Programming,** mid-Sixties graduate: "Living in a group situation (fraternity house). This gave me experience in coping/discovering many other types of personalities, exposed me to varied methods of studying and many other courses of study."

Some respondents who held a leadership position in their fraternity, sorority, or dormitory found that work required of the position also helped to develop their problem-solving, organizational, leadership, interpersonal, communications, and budgeting skills. Similar kinds of learning experiences were reported by persons who participated in activities such as student council, yearbook, newspaper, or dramatics.

> **Management Trainee,** mid-Seventies graduate: "Being sorority president for a group of 90 women exposed me to virtually all problems of management, though on a small scale. Trying to maintain morale, communications, and organization in the face of rising costs and competing interests was a real challenge for my creative insight and adaptability."

> **Bank Vice President,** mid-Sixties graduate: "In college, I held a number of jobs and was also treasurer and president of my fraternity. The former gave me insight into the business world and the latter the opportunity to lead."

> **Engineering Management Trainee,** mid-Seventies graduate: "Being managing editor of the newspaper helped . . . group coordination, leadership, authority, deadlines, exposure to work."

It appears that the college experience as a whole—just being away at college—was a strong influence in some cases. Being away from the protection of home, dealing with a large bureaucracy (though different from the bureaucracy of the working world), completing assignments, being in a competitive environment, all were cited as having a role in developing study and work habits, discipline, and maturity.

> **Transportation Engineer,** mid-Sixties graduate: "The experience that was gained in being away from the family environment and the necessity of making a majority of one's decisions in this environment was invaluable. It fostered the realization that the direction of my career was highly dependent on me."

> **Traffic Representative,** mid-Seventies graduate: "By going on to college it made me aware of other people, getting to know new friends and, in general, making me shift for myself by making me think and make my own decisions."

Another theme was the value of college activities for developing both teamwork and competitiveness. Among the activities cited were sports and special projects.

> **Vocational Placement Supervisor,** mid-Sixties graduate: "Sports and activities táught me team aspects of working as a unit."

> **Training Manager,** mid-Sixties graduate: "College football—instrumental in developing appreciation for organization, motivation, competitive urgency."

Previous studies have found an association between some measure of success on the job and participation in extracurricular activities during college or in group activities outside of work. Among 17,000 college graduates in the Bell Telephone System, those who had participated "substantially" in extracurricular activities while in college tended to earn higher salaries. In fact, such participation completely compensated for differences in the quality of college attended and partly compensated for differences in grades (American Telephone and Telegraph Company, 1962). Mahoney et al. (1961) also found that a group of "more effective" managers were differentiated from "less effective" managers on having been more involved in hobbies and sports. In another study of supervisors, those rated good or superior were most likely to spend their off hours in group activities, whereas those rated fair or poor tended to spend this time alone (Stockford, 1957).

What these studies left unknown was whether successful outcomes actually were influenced by extracurricular activities or whether participation in these activities was merely a common behavior of persons who are energetic, people-oriented, and competitive. However, the reports of respondents in the present study indicate that such participation does indeed strengthen a number of personal qualities and competencies—such as self-confidence, interpersonal skills, and leadership—that often are considered important for productive work.

Several studies in recent years have shown that campus living arrangements make a significant impact on academic outcomes. Living in a dormitory, in particular, has been associated with academic achievement and degree attainment (Astin, 1973; Chickering, 1974). Astin (1977) also found that membership in social fraternities or sororities significantly increased students' intellectual self-esteem and ambition. The reports of respondents to the present study help to tie these influences to careers by describing how the experience of living and cooperating with many different kinds of people, and the social and intellectual interchange it fostered, helped them relate to others on the job with greater self-confidence and understanding.

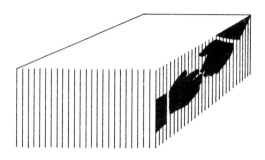

CHAPTER 4 **Considerations in Hiring**

Group Leader, Manufacturing R. & D., mid-Sixties graduate, majored in chemistry: "During an interview, it is easy to identify certain qualities and mannerisms in an individual just by how he conducts himself. This analysis can be done verbally without a college record to go by. Simply asking for a short discourse can give considerable insight into individual qualities. People are hired for their ultimate potential and not necessarily for their competence in the immediate task. The latter cannot be ignored completely, but it is not the overriding factor."

Financial Resources Administrator, mid-Sixties graduate, majored in accounting: "I feel that, up to a point, the job makes the person. Graduation from college is but one indication of potential. My ability to provide a work environment which will allow an individual to grow and fit within the structure is much more important than credentials or my initial impression."

Senior Research Chemist, mid-Sixties graduate: "The better a person has prepared himself educationally for his career, the greater his chance of success. In most industrial jobs it is better to have broad knowledge than deep knowledge. Beyond that, personality factors are most important. They must have a proper balance of aggressiveness and self-confidence. They must be organized and highly motivated. They should be flexible in the type of job they do and must have the ability and desire to gain the knowledge to do the new job. It is also important for a person to have the desire and ability to get along with a variety of types of people since most jobs require a person to interact with others and accomplish goals through others' work."

M OST LINE MANAGERS involved in the hiring process know the basic competency requirements of the particular position they are filling. They also can probably judge fairly well to what extent they can allow for training on the job and what competencies the candidate needs to possess initially. However, many hiring decisions must take into consideration the long-run value of the individual to the organization. Campus recruiters, who may interview large numbers of graduates for nonspecific assignments, often address the question of whether or not each candidate shows potential for growth on the job.

The findings described in the previous chapters indicate that the requirements of first and long-run jobs are not difficult to reconcile because of the process by which long-run competencies are acquired. Career development and increasing responsibilities lead to an expansion of the types of activities performed and competencies required, and many of these newly-required competencies are built upon or around the work performed earlier. Because the knowledge and skills for many of the long-run activities are learned on the job, it is valid in hiring new graduates to consider the needs of the first job plus potential, not actual, ability to perform higher level work. A concern for the new recruit as a long-run investment does not appear to necessitate hiring someone who is over-prepared or overqualified for the first job.

These conclusions are substantiated by responses to specific questions on factors to consider in hiring (*Table 20*). Respondents were asked to rate six criteria on their importance in deciding whether or not a new college graduate should be hired for the respondents' own career field:

- Prior work experience;
- General knowledge in a particular career area;
- Knowledge of how to perform the specific tasks involved in higher-level jobs;
- Relatedness of college major to job;
- College grades; and
- Potential for developing on the job.

They were asked also to indicate which of these criteria were taken into consideration when they themselves were hired for their first full-time job after graduation.

The most important criterion by far, in their view, was potential for future development on the job. Two-thirds of the mid-Sixties graduates and three-fourths of the mid-Seventies graduates believed that they were

TABLE 20

Factors in Hiring Decisions

(In percentages)

Factor	Believe Factor Was Consideration In Being Hired for First Full-Time Job	Importance That Should Be Given To Factor in Hiring Decision			
		Very Much	Moderate	Little	None
Graduates of Mid-Sixties					
Prior work experience	35	22	42	32	4
Knowledge in particular career area	39	22	59	18	1
Knowledge of how to perform specific tasks involved in higher level jobs	11	13	29	46	12
Relatedness of college major to job	51	28	46	23	2
College grades	39	16	68	13	2
Potential for developing on job	65	81	15	4	0
Graduates of Mid-Seventies					
Prior work experience	46	25	46	26	3
Knowledge in particular career area	47	32	48	17	3
Knowledge of how to perform specific tasks involved in higher level jobs	14	12	40	37	12
Relatedness of college major to job	54	29	43	22	5
College grades	56	12	63	22	3
Potential for developing on job	73	77	19	3	1

hired partly because of their potential for career growth, and 8 in 10 of both groups recommended that a great deal of importance be given to this criterion.

In the absence of other indicators, grades are often used in the selection process as an indicator of ability to achieve. From the responses to this survey, it seems that greater weight is being given to grades now than in the past. Fifty-six percent of the recent graduates, compared with 39 percent of the earlier graduates, attributed their being hired partly to college grades. However, very few (just 16 percent of mid-Sixties graduates and 12 percent of mid-Seventies graduates) felt that grades ought to be given more than moderate importance in the hiring decision.

Respondents were divided as to the importance of prior work experience, with almost half rating such experience as moderately important but with the other half almost equally split between high and little importance. However, they rejected the notion that graduates should be able to perform higher than entry-level functions. Clearly, they believed that the knowledge and skills to perform these functions should be acquired on the job.

Overall ratings of the importance of knowledge in the career area and relatedness of college major to one's job were somewhat higher than those for prior work experience. A large majority rated them at least moderately important. However, marked variations in the ratings were noted by occupation, particularly for relationship between college major and job (*Table 21*).

In most of the occupational areas included in this study, the majority of respondents did not consider a direct relationship between job and major essential. Engineers, scientists, and accountants were more likely than others to rate a relationship between major and job very important, but the largest proportion of any group to give this rating was 61 percent by accountants of the mid-Seventies. It seems that, even in jobs that require specific technical competencies, it is not the major field but the competencies themselves that are important. In many cases, the competencies can be acquired in a variety of ways, and knowing that someone majored in a field is no assurance that the competencies were acquired.

INDICATORS OF POTENTIAL FOR GROWTH

What constitutes potential for growth and development on the job? What characteristics should be used as indicators of this potential? In describing characteristics that would indicate potential for growth in their

TABLE 21 ───

Relation Between College Major and Job as Hiring Factor, by Current Occupation

Occupation	Graduates of Mid-Sixties Percent Who Rated This Factor Very Important	Graduates of Mid-Seventies Percent Who Rated This Factor Very Important
Engineer	33	46
Scientist	53	29
Computer specialist	15	33
Research/technology manager ..	36	13
Office work: manager or analyst .	19	15
Personnel officer	20	26
Accountant	48	61
Marketing specialist	11	13
Financial specialist	20	12

own career fields, respondents emphasized certain personal characteristics and attitudes, together with broadly-useful skills—especially interpersonal and communications skills (*Table 22*). Much less mention was made of specific knowledge and skill preparation. Administrative skills and other competencies which are important for long-range jobs, but are probably unnecessary for most first jobs, were rarely mentioned as indicators of potential. Such competencies are associated with growth rather than with potential.

Personal Qualities and Attitudes

Four types of positive attitudes were identified as essential ingredients of potential: (1) willingness to work well with others, to cooperate, to exhibit team spirit; (2) interest or enthusiasm about the work and field of work; (3) interest and enthusiasm regarding future development; and (4) willingness to learn.

> **Management Analyst,** mid-Seventies graduate, majored in accounting: "... confidence in self and abilities; interest in self-development; pleasant and agreeable personality; ambitious attitude, willingness to work at own development rather than to have it 'handed-out;' consciousness of needs of others, besides self."

TABLE 22 ————————————————————————————

Characteristics Indicating Potential for Growth

(In percentages)

Characteristics	Graduates of Mid-Sixties	Graduates of Mid-Seventies
Attitudes: cooperation, interest, enthusiasm, willingness to learn	61	52
Assertive qualities: independence, aggressiveness, self-confidence	45	45
Communications skills	30	20
Interpersonal skills	28	25
Intelligence, ability to learn, creativity	25	22
Knowledge, experience, technical skills	24	28
Grades, test scores	24	21
Work habits and organization	15	17
Major field of study (courses related to job)	10	10
Analytical, problem-solving skills	7	11
Rigor and breadth of college courses	7	2
Personal appearance	6	8
Administrative skills	5	1
Numerical, accounting skills	2	0
Patience, even-tempered nature	0+	2

Senior Sales Analyst, mid-Sixties graduate, majored in art: "Willingness to work at whatever is assigned—nothing is 'beneath him' or worthless since it will not apparently cause his promotion. Open-minded and flexible—there is not only one way to solve problems; people with other jobs coordinating with yours also have good ideas and your work helps or hinders theirs, not just your own."

Biologist, mid-Seventies graduate, majored in biology: ". . . an expression of wanting to continue education or to gain more skills, or an interest in and curiosity about all aspects of the job, and ability to get along with co-workers would be attitude characteristics for job development."

Often linked to these attitudes were various qualities of assertiveness: drive, ambition, aggressiveness, forcefulness, independence, initiative. As an indicator of assertiveness, some respondents would want to know whether or not the candidate had formulated goals. Participation in extracurricular activities also was cited as an indicator of potential by demonstrating sociability, energy, and drive. These comments were consistent with other opinions expressed regarding the relevancy of extracurricular activities for development of leadership.

Marketing Manager, mid-Sixties graduate, majored in social sciences: "Enthusiastic self-starter who will be able to ask and answer his or her own questions and learn concepts, products, etc. Indication of a competitive drive to excel—but still play the team game."

Buyer, mid-Sixties graduate, majored in business administration: "... People who work during college tend to be more organized, goal-oriented and aggressive, and the work helps prepare the graduate for a career. Eager to succeed, goal-oriented, aggressive, willing to work, hard worker, a doer, a planner. Self-confident."

Both ability to learn and willingness to learn were considered important. Grades were sometimes taken as an indicator of such ability. They were viewed also as an indicator of perseverance and good work habits. It seems, however, that respondents would not necessarily look for the highest grades, preferring instead to ascertain whether the candidate had maintained at least an average academic record. The "gentleman C" plus other characteristics (interest, drive, etc.) were considered more valuable in the long run than an A average without these characteristics.

Senior Compensation Analyst, mid-Seventies graduate, majored in psychology: "I would look for a college graduate with a proven track record of success. The graduate would have some prior work experience, good grades, extracurricular activities, and a generally good overall appearance. The graduate would have to be able to express a sincere desire for this employment and for achieving his ultimate career goal."

Computer Analyst, mid-Seventies graduate, majored in mathematics: "... Types of extracurricular activities the graduate was involved in and degree of involvement may give some indication of graduate's capacities and general enthusiasm. I don't think a GPA should be considered too heavily. However, passing a majority of courses with C, regardless of subject matter, may show the graduate has not only determination but also a sense of responsibility ..."

Personnel Officer, mid-Sixties graduate, majored in business: "Fairly good grades (though not necessarily outstanding grades). A general feeling for whether the person seemed bright, curious, and disciplined."

It seems that most respondents to this study would use the various common indicators—grades, college selectivity, and major field of study—with caution and only in combination with other information. The records of the mid-Sixties graduates who participated in this study are evidence to support the theory that good but not necessarily top grades are important. Three-fourths of the employer-designated productive college graduates in the mid-Sixties group reported grade averages between C+ and B. Only one in five reported B+ or better grades, but, on the other hand, only one in 17 averaged C or less.

Top grades may be overemphasized in the selection process today. Studies which have shown a positive relationship between grades and salary also have revealed that many "atypical" persons had low grades and high salary or high grades and low salary. Further, there is some doubt as to the meaning of the grades and salary relationship. Employers may offer higher salaries to persons with higher grades and, because these salaries become part of the permanent record, they create a continuing advantage. Such students also may be more likely to secure the fast-track jobs (Hoyt, 1965; H. Bowen, 1977). Recent publicity about "grade inflation" may diminish the value of high grades as an indicator of potential. At the same time, it may make employers less receptive to graduates with a "gentleman C."

Knowledge and Skills

Many references were made also to particular types of knowledge and skills which indicate potential for growth. Respondents tended to describe broadly-useful skills rather than occupationally-specific ones. Interpersonal and communications skills were emphasized. The *ability* to get along with and work well with others (distinct from *willingness* to do so, which was also mentioned) was considered useful for getting the job done and, eventually, for leadership. Among the communications skills, speaking and writing were considered especially important for writing letters and reports, conveying ideas, and persuading others.

> **Accountant,** mid-Seventies graduate: "The individual's ability to indicate his executive presence through personal contact."
>
> **Accountant,** mid-Seventies graduate: "Maturity, self-discipline, ability to get along with different people and situations, ambition, drive."
>
> **Chemist,** mid-Sixties graduate: "Ability to communicate with others, listen to others, share ideas. Flexibility, both in attitude and in work skills. Broad educational base—not too specialized."
>
> **Engineering Supervisor,** mid-Sixties graduate, majored in engineering: "Ability to communicate, creativity—from résumé or by conversation; motivation, logic, goal-setter, and achiever."

Some respondents also mentioned types of knowledge which they thought were indicative of potential—especially broad knowledge, combined with a demonstrated capacity to learn, as opposed to job-specific knowledge. Some preferred broadly-based individuals because they could be more flexible and fit into different situations. In fact, the words "flexible" or "versatile" were used by 24 respondents, referring both to attitude and knowledge base.

> **Accountant,** mid-Seventies graduate: "Enthusiasm to learn new things. Desire for 'success' (whatever or however you may define it). Ability to take on new responsibilities. General overall knowledge of area."

> **Chemical Engineer,** mid-Seventies graduate: "I would look for enthusiasm in the person concerning his or her experience in school and work. A person who expresses his or her ideas clearly and displays a versatile nature (i.e., the ability to function adequately in different job situations) would also be desirable. I would seriously consider a graduate who has adequate knowledge and works superbly with people as opposed to one with extensive knowledge who does not communicate or get along with people."

Growth Potential Indicators in Different Occupations

Despite the wide differences in the kind of work performed by respondents in the various occupations, there was a remarkable consensus with respect to the importance of positive attitudes such as interest, enthusiasm, willingness, and cooperation. All occupational groups ranked these attitudes as either first or second in importance in indicating potential for growth on the job (*Table 23*). Assertive qualities—aggressiveness, self-confidence, independence—were cited next most frequently across most occupational groups. Communications and interpersonal skills drew ratings in a moderate range.

However, the groups differed in a systematic way regarding the relative frequency with which they mentioned knowledge and skills, as opposed to ability to learn. Respondents in occupations having a specific knowledge base taught in college were more likely than others to mention knowledge and skills. "Computer specialist" is a case in point. Because of the newness of the field, fewer mid-Sixties graduates, compared with mid-Seventies graduates, had any college training in the computer field. Understandably, mid-Sixties graduates employed as computer specialists mentioned ability to learn more often than knowledge or experience, and mid-Seventies graduates in the same occupation mentioned knowledge more than ability to learn.

Grades were viewed as moderately important by most of the mid-Seventies groups and relatively unimportant by most of the mid-Sixties

TABLE 23

Rank Order of Seven Leading Characteristics Indicating Potential for Growth, by Current Occupation

Occupation	Attitudes	Assertive Qualities	Communications Skills	Interpersonal Skills	Ability to Learn, Intelligence	Knowledge, Skills	Grades
Graduates of Mid-Sixties							
Engineer	1	2	4	3	7	5-6	5-6
Scientist	1	2-3	5	2-3	7	4	6
Computer specialist	1	3-4	3-4	5-6	2	5-6	7
Research/technology manager	1	2	4	3	7	6	5
Office work: manager or analyst	1	7	2-4	5	6	2-4	2-4
Personnel officer	1	2-3	2-3	6	4	7	5
Accountant	1	2-3	4	6	7	5	2-3
Marketing specialist	1-2	1-2	7	4-5	3	4-5	6
Financial specialist	1	3	4-5	4-5	2	4-5	7
Graduates of Mid-Seventies							
Engineer	1	2	5	4	6	3	7
Scientist	1	2-4	7	2-4	5-6	5-6	2-4
Computer specialist	1	2-3	5-7	4	5-7	2-3	5-7
Research/technology manager	1-2	1-2	4-5	6-7	6-7	3	4-5
Office work: manager or analyst	1-2	1-2	4-5	6	5	3	4-5
Personnel officer	1-2	1-2	3	7	6	4-5	5-6
Accountant	2	1	7	3	4	5-6	5-6
Marketing specialist	1	2	5-7	5-7	3	4	5-7
Financial specialist	1	2	6	5	3-4	7	3-4

groups. As noted earlier, the mid-Sixties graduates had lower grades than the mid-Seventies graduates, and their own experiences may have influenced their attitude in this regard.

A CLASSIFICATION OF FACTORS IN HIRING

The factors described as important in the hiring decision and/or as indicating potential can be classified in four categories (*Figure 2*):

- Type A: Prerequisites—essential for effective performance on the first job and for advancement;
- Type B: Growth Promoters—valuable for the first job and for advancement;
- Type C: Additives—essential for some future jobs but usually acquired after college;
- Type D: Proxies—not inherently valuable, but used as indicators of other essential and valuable characteristics.

Prerequisites

Some characteristics were considered basic for good performance on the first job and also as foundations for future development. These included certain specific competencies which are required for entry-level functions and are not taught at the worksite. A job involving work with numbers would require basic competencies in mathematics, although specific applications of these competencies might be learned on the job. Effective work, in both entry-level and advanced capacities, was thought to depend on several factors: a knowledge base for further learning (particularly in occupations associated with a college major), ability to learn, and positive attitudes (interest, desire to learn, and willingness to work cooperatively with others).

Underlying many of the comments was the implied need for the individual to fit into the work environment. Two types of fit which were thought to be vitally important have been studied extensively. The fit between the individual's own vocational interests and the type of work performed has been a major focus of psychological research aimed at helping people make congruent and satisfying career choices (e.g., Holland, 1959, 1966). The fit between the individual's own style and values

FIGURE 2

Role of Various Factors in Hiring at Baccalaureate Level

	Knowledge, Skills, Attitudes, Qualities		
Type A Prerequisites	**Type B Growth Promoters**	**Type C Additives**	**Type D Proxies**
Specific competencies required but for which no on-the-job training is provided	Broad competencies	Administrative and leadership skills	College record
Knowledge base for on-the-job learning	Broad knowledge	Advanced knowledge and specialization	Extracurricular activities
Ability to learn	Broad interests		Work during college
Positive attitudes in a work situation	Interpersonal skills		Goals stated during interview
Fit between individual and type of work	Communications skills		Interest in continuing education expressed during interview
Fit between individual and organizational style	Assertiveness "to a degree"		Preparedness for interview
			"Chemistry"

and those of the organization in which he or she works also appears to be important for both job satisfaction and productivity (French, 1978).

Growth Promoters

Other characteristics were considered valuable but not essential; that is, they might make the difference between adequate and exceptional performance or between average and exceptional career development. Broad knowledge, skills, and interests were mentioned as factors indicating potential for growth on the job, and a broad knowledge base was described as valuable for adaptability, versatility, and learning the specific skills of new jobs as one advances.

Respondents thought that advancement was promoted by the ability to work well with people, express ideas well in writing and speaking, display self-confidence and aggressiveness ("up to a point"), and work independently. Further inquiry revealed that many respondents considered themselves somewhat deficient in these areas. Since they were selected for the survey by their employer on the basis of their productive work performance, it can be assumed that these deficiencies did not deter them from performing at least adequately. It is probable, however, that good interpersonal and communications skills are actually essential for some jobs.

Additives

Two types of knowledge and skills are classified as additives because they are necessary for some future jobs but are not considerations in hiring baccalaureates for entry-level jobs and are usually acquired at work. One is administrative skills. Many mid-Sixties graduates were employed in administration, but only one-third had learned to perform administrative functions in college. Also, few mentioned administrative skills as factors indicating potential.

Another additive is advanced skills and knowledge that may be required in future jobs. Some respondents felt that advanced but highly specialized and narrow knowledge might make the candidate less versatile and adaptable to new situations as they arise.

Proxies

There is some evidence that employers prefer to hire people with certain credentials, such as having achieved high college grades, attended a prestigious college, or majored in a particular field. These characteristics are used as proxies for the knowledge, skills, attitudes, and other qualities employers seek. Instead of basing their hiring decision on grades, some respondents emphasized extracurricular activities and prior work experience. Others emphasized qualities revealed in the interview situation—the candidate's formulation of career goals, interest in continued learning, and preparedness for the interview, as well as the overall impression of congeniality.

The importance given to an overall impression of congeniality, otherwise known as "chemistry," is a most human and natural response to an interview situation. No one wants to work closely with a disagreeable person. On the other hand, good "chemistry" is no assurance of good job performance and, whenever proxies are used, a distinction should be made between these experiences or achievements and the knowledge, skills, or personal qualities they ostensibly measure.

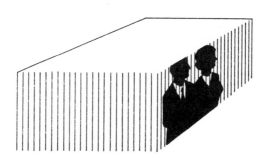

CHAPTER 5 **Considerations in Preparing for Work**

Management Recruiter, mid-Sixties graduate: "Any and all of the study areas may be considered most useful to the extent that they require logical, coherent thought."

Data Processing Systems Coordinator, mid-Sixties graduate: "The disciplined thought processes are important."

WHEN THINKING of college as a training ground for jobs, it is important to acknowledge that nearly half of the college students may change career plans during the first five or six years after graduation (Bisconti, 1975). Additional changes occur throughout a working life. Some career shifting may be attributed to inadequate counseling in the students' early years and lack of career awareness, but some can also be attributed to the nature of the world of work. The jobs available to college graduates are far too numerous and specialized for colleges to provide programs tailored to each. Jobs in business, industry, and government, which together employ a majority of those without advanced degrees, are especially difficult to keep track of and to classify. The catch-all title "business administrator" describes only in the broadest sense the variety of jobs it may encompass.

It is unlikely that many students today are preparing specifically for certain jobs held by respondents to this study, such as petroleum supply analyst or operations services manager or social security administrator. Newman (1975) even suggested the possibility that many of these "invisible careers" actually are nonexistent at the time students enroll in college. Moreover, the histories of the respondents to this study show that career development often involves substantial changes in or expansion of the functions performed on the job.

REFLECTIONS FROM HINDSIGHT

The fact that these graduates surveyed were performing their work effectively cannot be attributed to specific preparation in college for all their current work functions (see Chapter 2). But could they be performing their work even more effectively if they had taken different courses in college? Among those respondents who admitted to some work-related weakness, just half of the mid-Sixties group and one-third of the mid-Seventies group believed that these weaknessess could have been corrected by taking different or additional courses in college (*Table 24*). Many of those who did attribute weaknesses to some lack in their college studies would have changed or added a course or two but did not envision completely different study programs.

The primary weakness perceived, especially by the more recent graduates, was lack of experience in a particular area or need to refine

TABLE 24 ————————————————————————————

Assessment of Relation of College Courses to Current Work-Related Weaknesses

(In percentages)

Assessment	Graduates of Mid-Sixties	Graduates of Mid-Seventies
Weaknesses could have been corrected by taking different courses in college		
Yes	30	12
Yes, qualified (not different but more or additional)	18	22
Weaknesses could not have been corrected by taking different courses in college. . .	52	65

technical skills (*Table 25*). Such weaknesses, respondents felt, might have been overcome by taking more or different courses in their own scientific or technical field (*Table 26*).

Weaknesses related to work habits, work style, and attitudes were not considered amenable to change by taking particular college courses but required personal discipline and effort.

Improvement in generally applicable skill areas—communications, numerical (accounting, budgeting), administrative, and interpersonal—tended to be associated with taking courses outside one's field. Specific courses in speech, drama, and business writing were mentioned most often by people who majored in scientific fields and who perceived weaknesses in communications. Few mentioned more general English courses.

Further analyses of comments showed that improvement in administrative skills, including planning and decision-making, was associated with courses in business, particularly management, and improvement in accounting and budgeting was associated with courses in accounting and finance. Business, accounting, and finance courses were mentioned frequently by persons who majored in liberal arts and scientific fields and by persons who were currently involved in supervisory or managerial functions. More mentions of administrative and finance courses were made by mid-Sixties graduates. Mid-Seventies graduates, who were more likely to be involved in technical than administrative functions, tended to focus on technical weaknesses.

Why didn't respondents take these courses that might have helped? To some extent they were constrained by their perceptions of educational or employment policies (*Table 27*). Some college programs permitted few elective courses and/or did not recommend the areas that might have helped. A small number of respondents, because of their perception regarding the strong emphasis employers place on grades, avoided taking courses that might have helped but seemed difficult. Their fear of poor grades was greater than their desire to overcome what they already knew to be a weakness. Other respondents missed taking the courses because such courses were not offered at their campus or, simply, because they were not aware of the usefulness of the subject matter.

RECOMMENDATIONS TO CURRENT AND FUTURE STUDENTS

As a guide to current and future students, respondents recommended study areas that would be useful to persons preparing for jobs like theirs.

TABLE 25 ————————————————————————————————

Assessment of Work-Related Weaknesses

(In percentages)

Weakness	Graduates of Mid-Sixties	Graduates of Mid-Seventies
Skills needing improvements:		
Analytical	2	2
Communications	20	14
Interpersonal	9	7
Administrative	11	7
Numerical (primarily accounting, budgeting)	14	3
Need more experience, refine techniques	24	39
Poor work habits, disorganized, proscrastinate	17	13
Impatient with incompetent subordinates, bureaucracy, superiors, etc.	10	9
Lack interest, bored with job or some aspect of it, detail work	9	9
Not assertive enough, too much of a nice guy	8	13
Not innovative enough	3	1
Lack advanced degree	3	2
Too assertive, too aggressive	2	2

TABLE 26 ————————————————————————————————

Assessment of Courses That Would Have Corrected Weaknesses

(In percentages)

Course	Graduates of Mid-Sixties	Graduates of Mid-Seventies
Business, management	25	19
Accounting, finance, mathematics	29	14
Economics	9	7
Other business—personnel, marketing ..	11	9
Communications—speech, drama, business writing	25	26
English	4	9
Specialized courses in own scientific field	17	32
Psychology, sociology, human relations ..	11	7
Other liberal arts—philosophy, political science	4	3
Other—law, computer programming	4	5

TABLE 27 _____

Reasons for Not Taking Courses That Could Have Corrected Weaknesses

(In percentages)

Reason	Graduates of Mid-Sixties	Graduates of Mid-Seventies
Didn't know they would be useful	26	13
Had to concentrate in own field, had few electives	23	40
Not offered, not aware they were offered	23	16
Didn't like subject, not interested	13	11
Didn't plan this type of work, had different interests then	11	8
Difficult, afraid of getting low grades	8	8
Not recommended or required	7	4
Had not defined career objectives	2	8
Thought these courses were only for career specialists	1	2
Courses in areas were not helpful	1	2
No value for finding job	1	0
Kept putting it off	1	0
Professor was notoriously bad	0	2
Don't know	2	1

Eighteen study areas were listed on the questionnaire, replicating a similar question included in the Bisconti and Solmon (1976) survey. The question was also used in a concurrent followup of more recent graduates (Ochsner and Solmon, 1979). The results of all three surveys showed that six study areas were outstanding, not only for frequency of mention but also for their general applicability across occupations: English, business administration, mathematics, economics, psychology, and accounting (*Table 28*).

In the present survey, the questionnaire provided space for respondents to indicate a maximum of three study areas that they considered *most* useful. It was hypothesized that certain subject areas, such as English and psychology, which had been checked as useful by large numbers of persons in the earlier study, might be generally applicable but considered relatively unimportant compared with some less generally applicable fields. However, the additional measure of level of importance actually showed that those areas mentioned most frequently also were considered to be of high relative value.

TABLE 28 _____

Study Areas Recommended for Own Type of Work

(In percentages)

Study Area	Area Is Useful		Area Is One of Most Useful	
	Graduates of Mid-Sixties	Graduates of Mid-Seventies	Graduates of Mid-Sixties	Graduates of Mid-Seventies
English	78	66	48	39
Languages	9	10	2	2
Other arts and humanities	22	18	6	5
Economics	67	53	21	19
Sociology	28	20	8	7
Psychology	54	46	21	21
History	11	7	4	1
Other social sciences	17	13	2	3
Biological sciences	10	9	4	3
Mathematics	62	65	25	37
Chemistry	25	24	8	13
Physics	25	27	6	8
Other physical sciences ..	8	6	1	2
Accounting	52	45	26	21
Business administration ..	77	64	50	39
Other business	40	40	16	14
Education	6	4	4	1
Engineering	34	39	26	35

Note: Eighteen study areas were listed. Additional recommendations written in the "other" blank were: computer programming (44 mentions), communications including speaking (30 mentions), law (12 mentions), and other miscellaneous areas. Marketing, finance, insurance, and public relations were grouped with "other business;" human behavior was grouped with psychology.

English and business administration both were recommended by three-fourths of the mid-Sixties graduates and two-thirds of the mid-Seventies graduates. Further, they were selected among the three most useful study areas by half the earlier graduates and 4 in 10 of the more recent group. Mathematics, economics, psychology, and accounting also maintained their high rank among study areas when respondents selected the most important fields.

The potential role of English, mathematics, economics, psychology and business administration as core subjects in a work-relevant curriculum is indicated by the consistency with which they were mentioned across occupations (*Tables A-3 and A-4*). The most consistently selected study area was English; among all nine occupational groups, it ranked fourth or higher in frequency of mentions. Business-related courses and mathematics were also rated consistently high by most occupational groups, while psychology and economics received more middling ratings. Natural science and engineering courses were rarely recommended except by those in scientific and engineering occupations.

In attempting to explain the predominance of English and, to a lesser degree, psychology among recommended courses, Bisconti and Solmon (1976, p. 36) suggested:

> "It is probably not the knowledge of medieval poetry or the ability to conduct experiments with rats to which these recommendations refer, but rather the tools for writing reports or memos and the ability to get along with and manage people."

One of the objectives of the present study was to find out from respondents directly why they recommended particular study areas, in order to ascertain how the study areas are perceived to relate to work.

English

It was observed earlier in this chapter that, when respondents were asked about courses that might have corrected their weaknesses, they tended to refer to communications courses rather than English. Further, although communications was not one of the 18 study areas listed in the question on recommendations, 30 respondents wrote it into the space provided for "other" areas.

The main thrust of respondents explanations for their recommendation of English was, in fact, their perceived need for good communications skills on the job. Six in 10 of those who recommended this area actually used the word communications or communicate. They saw communications as a constant and vital part of the job and frequently referred to practical applications of the ability to speak and write well. Especially important to all occupational groups was the meaningful presentation of ideas in report form.

> **Auto Safety Engineer,** mid-Sixties graduate: "My job is to present the results of engineering analyses or tests to nonengineering persons . . . businessmen, lawyers, judges, government regulators, etc. The most brilliant engineer in the world is useless if no one can understand him."

> **Chemist,** mid-Sixties graduate: "No matter how clever the scientist, sooner or later he has to communicate what he has done to colleagues, sponsors, the government, etc. It helps if he can read and write his own language."

> **Chemical Engineer,** mid-Seventies graduate: "If one can't communicate the engineering and economic reasons for building his engineering marvel, then he'll lead a very frustrating life."

Those in business frequently referred to the need to communicate with clients, to write letters and memos. Some commented that they were referring specifically to business-related English courses, such as business letter writing.

> **Budget and Personnel Manager,** mid-Sixties graduate: "Contributes to effective communication. However, a more useful orientation would have been something like 'Business English'."

Respondents, especially accountants, repeatedly described the need for reports to be "clear and concise."

> **Finance and Auditing Manager,** mid-Sixties graduate: "Report writing in a clear, concise, and grammatical style is important in almost any business field, but particularly important in mine."

> **Auditor,** mid-Seventies graduate: "Clear, concise oral and written expression is imperative in the accounting profession."

Another point stressed by some was the value of English for promoting logical and critical thinking. This discipline was thought to assist not only in communicating but also in understanding what others have written.

> **Production Chemist,** mid-Seventies graduate: "It is important to be able to write thoughts very well. One needs to read critically and with great understanding."

Several mid-Sixties graduates expressed dismay over what they perceived to be a deterioration in the preparation of students to communicate.

> **Personnel Manager,** mid-Sixties graduate: "Communications is vital—is currently in a state of deterioration. College grads can no longer write complete sentences or spell or even speak through a complete thought."

Other Arts and Humanities

Although other arts and humanities courses were recommended much less frequently than English, they were seen as helping to develop a well-rounded, interesting person. Some respondents believed that a humanistic background was helpful on the job, not only for presentation of one's self but also for understanding and appreciating others.

> **Branch Manager,** mid-Sixties graduate: "Helps to understand and appreciate ourselves and others."

> **Computer Programmer,** mid-Sixties graduate: "All programming builds logical flow of ideas—must be able to understand intersection and union of sets and default type logic."

Psychology and Other Social Sciences

Psychology was viewed as a key to the understanding of people, an essential element in interpersonal skills and effective job performance. As reported in previous chapters, interpersonal skills are important, even in occupations that are traditionally thought to be oriented toward "things" rather than "people." This was demonstrated by the fact that moderate proportions of most occupational groups placed psychology in the top three recommended study areas.

Some respondents related an understanding of others to counseling and human development functions; others spoke of channeling behavior to meet corporate goals. Psychology was seen as important for improving one's ability to get along with and deal with both fellow employees and clients. It was associated particularly with handling problem situations and was considered critically important for those in supervisory positions.

> **Executive Director, Nonprofit Organization,** mid-Sixties graduate: "Helps develop a better feel for people—their problems, concerns. Significant amount of counseling."

> **Research Manager,** mid-Sixties graduate: "Most of the work is done by others. It is very necessary to understand them and their needs in order to provide a proper environment to excel."

> **Industrial Relations Specialist,** mid-Sixties graduate: "Knowledge of human behavior assists in properly channeling the efforts of others."

> **General Supervisor,** mid-Sixties graduate, majored in engineering: "An understanding of why people react could enable me to better direct their energies toward job goals."

> **Mechanical Engineer,** mid-Sixties graduate: "A person who
> doesn't understand people and can't work with them is handi-
> capped. An engineer works with supervisor, other engineers,
> draftsmen, shop people, production people, and customers."

The same theme—need for understanding and getting along with
others—was given as a reason by the smaller number recommending other
social science disciplines, chiefly sociology. However, two other elements
were associated more with sociology than with psychology: a societal
perspective and methodologies of investigation and analysis.

> **Executive Director,** mid-Sixties graduate: "Must understand the
> major components of the society as we must collaborate with all of
> them to provide relevant services."
>
> **Engineer,** mid-Seventies graduate: "Ethics course would be help-
> ful in forming a better attitude toward work and society."
>
> **Marketing Manager,** mid-Sixties graduate: "No specific connec-
> tion with my job but the process of gathering information and assim-
> ilating is the same and is an excellent base."

Business Administration

Business administration was the area most frequently recommended
by office managers and analysts, personnel specialists, and marketing
specialists because of the direct applicability of business principles and
procedures to their jobs. It was also an important study area for re-
search/technology managers, accountants, and financial specialists. Many
respondents considered a broad knowledge of the business world, including general business practices and organizational structures, a prerequisite for getting along in the corporate environment.

> **Data Processing Supervisor,** mid-Sixties graduate: "A general
> knowledge of business and the priorities thereof helps one to adapt
> to the realities of the business world."
>
> **Management Trainee (Personnel),** mid-Seventies graduate: "To
> provide a basic understanding of the business world, profit motive,
> management techniques, familiarity with business-related legal de-
> cisions."
>
> **College Recruiter,** mid-Seventies graduate: "Every job, no matter
> what type, functions on a business-like basis and everyone needs to
> understand basics."
>
> **Engineering Assistant,** mid-Seventies graduate: "A general un-
> derstanding of business administration and organizational interde-

pendence should help a new hire comprehend his relative position in a corporation."

Part of functioning within this environment apparently involves understanding the "language" of business and penetrating the inner circle of those with strong business training.

> **Engineer,** mid-Sixties graduate: "Accountants and business majors have their sphere of influence—somewhat difficult to understand/penetrate."

For some, this understanding of the business world and organizational structure was seen as a basis for career development and further learning on the job.

> **Engineer,** mid-Sixties graduate: "If you expect to move up in a company, you must understand basis of how business operates, measure effectiveness, etc."

> **Engineer,** mid-Sixties graduate: "Organizational structure, management, budgeting are important abilities for advancement to upper level positions."

Another frequent theme was the need for an understanding of business principles in order to perform management functions effectively and to become a good leader and decision-maker. Some related this concept to the training in decision-making and problem-solving received in business administration courses through the case study and other techniques.

> **Investment Analyst,** mid-Sixties graduate: "By analyzing various case studies, it proves one's ability to analyze current situations."

> **Manager of Materials,** mid-Sixties graduate: "Development of your thought process and discipline to identify, analyze, and solve problems and make good decisions."

A few respondents in scientific fields pointed out the need to relate scientific and technical decisions and products to corporate goals. Others mentioned that awareness of all aspects of company operations, which is promoted by broad familiarity with business subjects, enables persons employed in large organizations to make useful contributions to other divisions and components.

> **Turn Foreman,** mid-Seventies graduate: "The cost analysis or de-

velopment of a particular product—when it becomes profitable to make it or to remove it."

Personnel Planning Specialist, mid-Sixties graduate: "Broad knowledge of enterprise so as to understand what you can contribute."

Financial Analyst, mid-Seventies graduate: "This will give you a feel for the interrelationships of the various departments and what information is helpful to the various departments."

Economics

Whereas business administration was viewed as a practical basis for many jobs, economics was viewed as a theoretical basis. It was quite important to financial specialists and moderately so to most other occupational groups except scientists and computer specialists.

Some respondents linked economics in a general way to their jobs, describing the dependence on cost control and/or profits.

Senior Account Representative, mid-Sixties graduate: "Business is governed by economics."

Manager of Import Traffic Department, mid-Sixties graduate: "We deal in costs, and an understanding of economics is necessary and useful."

Others referred to economic theories, concepts, or methodologies and to the value of the discipline for problem-solving.

Senior Buyer, mid-Seventies graduate: "Ability to study trends and cycles to determine how, when, and where to buy goods and/or services."

Accountant, mid-Sixties graduate: "The theoretical basis of supply and demand, conglomerates, U.S. government purchases, practices, policies, and their impact on society and business must be appreciated."

Section Manager, Data Processing, mid-Sixties graduate: "Provides overview of integrated business relationships—finance, production, etc. Discipline is good for developing problem identification and analysis skills."

Accounting

Accounting was recommended primarily by persons in business-related occupations. Almost all accountants stated, quite simply, that a sound educational preparation in accounting is a prerequisite for entry into the field.

> **Accountant,** mid-Sixties graduate: "Accounting and auditing are the foundations of my profession and sound, fundamental knowledge is required."

> **Accountant,** mid-Seventies graduate: "In my field, technical competence is absolutely essential. Accounting courses are the only source of such technical knowledge."

Mathematics

Mathematics, like English and psychology, was viewed as a fundamental work-related discipline which provides basic tools. Reiterated, particularly by respondents in scientific and engineering fields, was the theme that mathematics is both the queen and servant of all the other sciences.

> **Hydrologist,** mid-Sixties graduate: "All science fields use mathematics as a language. Easy to understand other sciences and highly related to computer sciences as used within my job."

> **Lead Project Engineer,** mid-Seventies graduate: "The universal language and common bond of the sciences. It is based on logic, truth, and discipline."

> **Engineer,** mid-Seventies graduate: "You can't be an engineer without it."

Study of mathematics was considered valuable also as a means of sharpening the thought processes.

> **Suggestions Investigator,** mid-Seventies graduate: "The logic and discipline required for rational problem-solving."

Various practical business applications of mathematics were described, such as report writing, budgeting, pricing, calculating claim benefits, and making projections. Several respondents mentioned that, when one needs to perform calculations accurately in the presence of clients, complete confidence with numbers is essential. In addition, the mathematics discipline was seen as a key to understanding reports and interpreting data.

> **Banker,** mid-Sixties graduate: "The business is one of rates and prices. Necessarily a facility with numbers and number manipulations is the key."

> **Catalog Control Buyer,** mid-Seventies graduate: "Financially, all
> jobs will rotate around figures. Confidence in numbers is important
> in everyday transactions."

Engineering and Natural Sciences

Comments regarding the value of engineering and natural science
courses to people entering related occupations are summed up by an engineer, a graduate of the mid-Sixties, who said: "Provides necessary
background and teaches a person to think logically."

Some respondents stressed the technical background. Others stressed
logic and discipline. Some, like the engineer quoted above, stressed both.
Natural sciences and engineering were considered essential for obtaining
basic knowledge in a related occupational field. The sciences were
considered fundamental areas also as a background for understanding
the basic principles of engineering.

For jobs in industry, both engineers and scientists tended to stress
breadth, rather than specialization, coupled with a good grounding in
methodology and problem-solving approaches.

> **Chemist,** mid-Sixties graduate: "The changing job market has
> made it very difficult to enter a narrow scientific discipline and expect to be able to stay there for a full working lifetime—about 40
> years. Witness the boom to bust change in the aerospace field over
> a span of less than five years. More and more big companies are
> looking for fewer and fewer people with a computer-like knowledge
> of a single subject area; they feel that a bright, flexible person who
> can go in different directions as social needs and pressures change is
> the best bet, particularly since so much practical training has to be
> done on the job anyway. My advice is to get as diverse a course
> background as possible while concentrating on your major field.
> Adaptability and survival in science may be synonymous."

MAKING THE MOST OF THE COLLEGE YEARS

College education cannot be expected to provide all of the knowledge
and skills required for all of the jobs into which college graduates may
enter, because jobs, job functions, and people are in constant flux. Part
of the preparation for work is understanding how the college experience
contributes to work performance so that the student not only can select
courses carefully but can relate the knowledge and skills acquired in these
courses to work requirements. Toombs (1974) pointed out that this
process is both an education for the student and a self-promotion tool.

Obviously, the amount of broad-technical and specialized-technical preparation students should have depends on the type of work they may take on after graduation and requires careful planning and counseling. Plans may change, and an engineering graduate may decide to go into a business job, but a graduate without a background in engineering or physics is highly unlikely to enter an engineering career. The same pattern is true for accountants and scientists. Persons with a background in a technical area, if reasonably well-rounded, have more options because they can enter jobs requiring no specific training, whereas persons with no specific training rarely can enter jobs in technical areas.

Baccalaureates in science and technology who plan careers in business and industry may take note of the experiences and recommendations of engineers and scientists who responded to this survey. Emphasized were breadth of knowledge, grounding in methodology, good reasoning and problem-solving approaches, and the ability to learn.

Further, although these occupations traditionally are associated with things rather than people, engineers and scientists in the sample frequently pointed out the importance of liberal arts courses, especially English for communicating with others (speaking and writing) and psychology for interpersonal skills (understanding, counseling, and leading). They also suggested that a scientist who enters a large organization may benefit from business administration courses for adaptation to the environment and for facilitating advancement to and functioning in managerial positions.

On the other hand, not everyone can or should concentrate in technical areas. For many of the first and future jobs in which college graduates may become employed, specific knowledge is not as important as a general knowledge base and good preparation for learning, thinking, and solving problems. This kind of preparation and discipline can be acquired in any field of college study.

Reviewing the comments of respondents, it is striking that one of the explanations given by at least some respondents for practically every recommended study area was that the area teaches one to think logically. This holds true for history, philosophy, and political science just as it does for business administration, accounting, chemistry, and engineering.

A history major who, by 1975, had become branch manager of an insurance company offered the following general advice:

"It is my opinion that an excellent liberal arts education would enable one to become an educated person. A well-educated person who is well disciplined and willing to work hard can do well in my occupational area. The ability to think independently, communicate effectively, and to define and solve problems is a must."

Some respondents, in their general comments, advised students to select a major field of study that really interests them. In order to profit from any course of study, they pointed out, it is necessary for the student to be interested and challenged.

> **Advertising Manager,** mid-Sixties graduate: "Study hard. Major in whatever field you like because that is where you'll develop the skills needed to succeed."

> **Engineer-Supervisor,** mid-Sixties graduate: "Enjoy what you're learning at least 50 percent of the time—if you can't, switch your major!!!"

Regardless of major area of study, respondents advised good use of elective courses, taking, as one computer programmer put it, "a full range of courses so you may be able to use your courses to enjoy your career and function well in every aspect of your life."

And, in every course, the student, they felt, could benefit greatly from probing beyond the "what?" and posing frequently the question "why?"

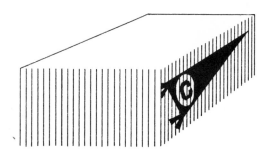

CHAPTER 6 **College Education in Perspective**

THE SPREADING suspicion that colleges and universities are failing in the career preparation aspects of their mission has resulted in an unfavorable climate for education. This climate is manifested by cutbacks in appropriations to education and by the growth of legislation designed to protect students as consumers and to foster choices by students of study areas associated with careers in high demand and high-income fields.

The purpose of this study was not to evaluate colleges and universities with respect to career-preparation goals but rather to describe work-relevant college experiences and put them in perspective. The responses of two groups of graduates, both selected by their employers because of their effective performance on the job, indicate that the work-related benefits of college do not occur in isolation. They build on earlier life experiences and provide a foundation for further growth. A wide variety of college experiences—both in and out of the classroom—can enhance work effectiveness in many ways.

THE ROLE OF COLLEGES AND UNIVERSITIES

Assessments of the college contribution to work have focused largely on two student outcomes: finding a "good" job and becoming employed in an occupation related to one's major. This view of what the college experience has to offer is far too narrow. It places on colleges and universities responsibilities that are only to a limited extent theirs and fails to emphasize more important job-related goals.

How the College Years Fit In

Respondents to this study viewed college as one of the many stepping stones to competent performance of work. Looking back on the development of the skills and knowledge required to perform their work effectively, early influences were recognized. Home, school, and jobs all played a role in the early formation of vocational interests and qualities which respondents considered basic and indispensable, such as a sense of responsibility and disciplined thinking. Projects, hobbies, chores, and parental guidance were cited as part of these developmental experiences.

College education, for many, provided the knowledge base in an occupational field. A more extensive contribution, however, was the development of analytical and problem-solving abilities. Some of the jobs held by respondents required a solid grounding in the principles and processes of a field. But even for these jobs, an important college contribution was the formation of the basic knowledge required to learn more on the job. Respondents found this role of college education appropriate because they believed that the nature of the work necessitated continued on-the-job learning. Most respondents, even in occupations such as engineer or accountant, developed a major part of their job knowledge after college.

As years go by and people progress in their careers, the contribution of college to current work may seem to diminish. The findings of this study indicate that the absolute contribution often has not diminished. Rather, new and expanded work functions have been added to those for which the college education, in many instances, provided a base, and thus the contribution of college education relative to that of on-the-job learning grows somewhat smaller.

The histories of the respondents in this study indicate that college education is more likely to prepare people for the kinds of work activities they perform on the first or early job than for those they perform as they advance in their career. Again, respondents believe that this was appropriate because of the difficulty of predicting the requirements of advanced positions and because of on-the-job learning.

The contributions of college education to work that appear to have the most lasting impact are those frequently overlooked in examining education-work relationships. In addition to basic knowledge of a field and broad general knowledge, they include logical thinking and problem-solving skills, communications skills, interpersonal skills, and a sensitivity to different kinds of people.

How Nonacademic Experiences Contribute

The narrow approach to assessing the college contribution neglects the fact that much important learning for work takes place outside the classroom. The rewards from various experiences—participation in team sports; living in a dormitory, fraternity, or sorority; active involvement in student government and in other leadership roles—may not wholly justify the investment in a college education, but they do represent an important dividend.

For many respondents to this study, extracurricular activities helped to develop interpersonal and leadership skills and self-confidence. One of the benefits of participating in sports was learning the combination of teamwork and competitiveness, a combination which was thought to promote career development and effective performance on the job. Living on campus and participating in extracurricular experiences benefited respondents by bringing them into close contact with people from different backgrounds and with different views.

How Academic Experiences Contribute

It is well documented that the details learned in college courses are soon forgotten. What remains is more likely to be general knowledge, broad principles, and concepts. Bowen (1977) reached this conclusion after reviewing a large number of studies. His review also revealed a variety of ways in which college education contributes to cognitive development, including "verbal skills," "intellectual tolerance," and "esthetic sensibility" (Bowen, 1977, p. 98). Other studies have found that college education contributes to further learning by providing the background for later development in a field (Pace, 1974) and helping to develop the skills to learn more efficiently (Rosen, 1975).

The comments of respondents to the present study link these educational outcomes to work. Respondents stressed the need on the job for a solid knowledge base as a foundation for further learning. The vast majority felt that college courses contributed in developing this foundation. Engineers, scientists, and accountants were more likely than others to find that the facts learned in college courses were useful on the job, but even these groups valued general concepts and principles and breadth. Even in the most technical occupations, the dynamic nature of careers and the need for continued learning was evident.

One of the most significant contributions of a college education, in the opinion of these respondents, is the development of analytical skills. Logical thinking was considered an asset for all occupations represented in the study, and its development was thought to be promoted by a wide range of college disciplines.

Respondents further substantiated the conclusions of Bisconti and Solmon (1976) and Ochsner and Solmon (1979) that liberal arts courses, particularly English and psychology, have direct applicability to work. Some of the general competencies they may build, including communications skills and understanding of people, were considered very important, even essential, for work.

Nevertheless, there appears to be a disconcerting trend to de-emphasize these subjects in the college curriculum. Catalogs published by 271 sample institutions between 1966–67 and 1973–74 showed that the portion of the curriculum allotted to general education requirements, including English and mathematics, had decreased (Blackburn et al., 1976). However, the recent approval of curriculum changes at Harvard, emphasizing more stringent general education requirements and basic proficiency in expository writing, mathematics, and foreign languages, may signal a rebirth of the parts of college study that were so heavily emphasized by respondents to this study.

A strong conclusion from the results of the present study is that de-emphasizing general education, English, and mathematics will not serve to increase graduates' effectiveness on the job. This conclusion is supported by earlier studies as well. In one earlier study, executives explained the failure of low-achieving subordinate executives as being due, above all, to overspecialization. Other weaknesses were noted also in interpersonal, analytical, and managerial skills (Gaudet and Carli, 1957). Similarly, a survey of employers in Washington County, Tennessee, identified five areas of deficiency in the work force there. Heading the list were basic communications, mathematics, and practical human relations skills (Hardin, 1973).

Perhaps the fall from grace experienced by English, mathematics, and general education during recent years can be attributed more to lack of awareness of how the subject matter can develop work-related competencies than to an inherent lack of relevance.   One corrective approach would be to look for career relevance in the traditional subject matter, rather than discard it.   A recent Houghton Mifflin series in career education provides some beginning conceptualization for such an approach (Rutan and Wilson, 1975).

THE ROLE OF STUDENTS

The profit to be gained from college education depends not only on the colleges but also on the students themselves.   Their selection of courses, their approach to learning, and their ability to capitalize on what they have learned will all have some effect on their eventual employability and career progress.

Developing Flexibility

A major theme to emerge from this study was the importance of flexibility and adaptability.   Respondents often recommended the establishment of a solid base in a field but counseled against overspecialization.

Many career development experts now believe that overspecialization may reduce one's options and limit the possibility of making choices that best fit one's interest, values, abilities, self-concept, and changing needs. Psychologists once believed that a single right job existed for each person (Parsons, 1909).   Now, psychological theories and instruments reflect the belief that a wide range of jobs within particular categories may fit an individual's personal characteristics.

Holland's extensively used and studied instrument, the Self-Directed Search, is designed to help people identify suitable groups of occupations. It advises that "it is usually best to defer making a single, specific occupational choice until it is absolutely necessary; if one can prepare himself for several related occupations simultaneously, his final selection will have a better chance of fitting his abilities and personality."

Similarly, much work in developmental theory has stressed Ginzberg's early concept of an irreversible process of career choice occurring in stages and ending when a final commitment is made.   However, Ginzberg himself now views the process as a more dynamic one occurring throughout life.   Although he still believes that decisions affect choices in a cumulative way, he no longer views the process as irreversible and feels that the principal challenge today is keeping one's options open (Ginzberg, 1972). The theories imply that better fit will lead to more effective work and that better fit can be achieved by avoiding a narrow commitment.

The principle of developing job-related competencies while maintaining job options is reflected in recent curriculum models that organize the curriculum in relation to clusters of careers having some commonalities in skill requirements (e.g., Maley, 1975). These models do not treat academic subjects, such as English, mathematics, and science, as separate units. Instead, they relate aspects of these subjects to clusters of jobs in skill families. The emphasis is on the development of skills to solve work problems rather than on the selection of, or preparation for, single occupations. From such schemes, it is possible to see a range of applications for particular curriculum areas, as well as a range of job possibilities for persons who develop particular sets of skills.

Utilizing Educational Resources Effectively

Major, minor, or elective courses can be used to develop basic work-related competencies that are applicable to many different occupations. English or communications courses may contribute to the ability to write effectively. Basic writing was thought necessary for many jobs, and English, along with business administration, was the most frequently recommended study area. As one advances, communication of ideas in report form becomes increasingly important. In fact, the contribution of college education to communications skills may become increasingly apparent with years on the job.

The importance of psychology for interpersonal skills was frequently stressed. Respondents mentioned the need to understand people in order to work cooperatively. As managers, they recommended psychology for directing the work efforts of one's subordinates towards corporate goals and for helping them to develop fully. Mathematics, too, appears to be a broadly relevant tool—for everyday calculations, as the basis for performing scientific analysis, and for understanding reports. Further, business administration and economics courses may be widely applicable and of particular value to anyone who might enter a large corporation or organization, either public or private.

The findings of this study support Cross' Learning Model which stresses the development of broad competencies (Cross, 1976 a and b). Further, respondents support her conceptualization regarding the role of communications, interpersonal, numerical, and administrative skills. Their statements confirm the value of emphasizing human relations ability and cooperative problem-solving.

The histories of the college graduates studied showed that the educational resources of the college campus extend beyond the classroom. Students can improve their employment and career potential by taking an active part in extracurricular activities that develop cooperative behavior, self-confidence, and leadership. Work during the college years was invaluable to many of the respondents, even if not related to later employment.

All of the college experiences may contribute in some way. With the help of good counseling, a student should be able to identify the potential applicability to work of courses such as philosophy, languages, and geography. Students can then direct their studies in these courses toward maximizing work-relevant aspects and can use this knowledge in presenting qualifications to prospective employers.

Respondents' comments and advice to students indicated that interest is a key to profiting from one's studies and enjoying and developing in a career. Their responses suggested further that, unless the occupation requires a certain field of preparation, the major assets—other than attitudes—that a student can bring from college to work are a general knowledge base and the ability to think and learn. Such assets can be developed in any field of study if the student applies himself or herself to the studies appropriately. Respondents stressed hard work, outside reading, and frequently asking "why?"

The Role of Employers

Contrary to popular belief, the major training ground for jobs is not the university but the work setting. Job training is a basic and continuing part of career development. Although most training is informal (including simply learning by doing), many employers offer formal training programs. French (1977) reported that 83 percent of the large firms (5,000 or more employees) offer formal training programs. Mincer (1962) estimated, for men, that the personal investment in on-the-job training (foregone earnings) was equal to the investment in formal education.

Historically, increased education has not been a substitute for on-the-job training. Between 1939 and the early 1960s, investments in formal education rose dramatically. During the same period, measurable investments in on-the-job training also increased (Mincer, 1962). For an individual, spending more time in school has not reduced the amount of subsequent investment in on-the-job training. On the contrary, more years of schooling has been associated with higher investments in on-the-job training (Mincer, 1962; Becker, 1964).

Bowman (1965), in an historical analysis, found that the stimulation and maintenance of rapid economic growth has depended on simultaneous rises in education and on-the-job training. As the pace of economic change increases, specialized skills rapidly become obsolete, and on-the-job training and retraining become increasingly important. Bowman and other economists (e.g., Weisbrod, 1962) believe that higher levels of schooling in general skills provide the flexibility to benefit more from on-the-job training and to adapt to changing work requirements.

Respondents to this study stressed that the kind of person who would have potential for job development in their occupations was not one who already possessed specialized or advanced skills but who was trainable and flexible. No matter how much the occupation was related to an academic discipline, respondents acquired a substantial portion of their job knowledge at work.

Improving Articulation Between Education and Work-Based Job Learning

In much of the writing and discussion today regarding the failure of higher education to prepare college graduates for work, there seems to be an implicit assumption that changes in the educational system could have the capability of curing any number of real or imagined work-related social ills: unemployment, underemployment, low productivity, worker dissatisfaction, absenteeism, turnover, mental illness, and so on.

The employer role in the process of preparing people for work has not been neglected altogether, but the major focus has been on the employer as an instrument for changing or bolstering the educational system rather than on the employment setting as the primary training ground. Resolutions to discontinuities between college education and work have been sought less in the human resource development function than in the expanded employer function as provider of work experience to students, lecturer on campus, curriculum planning consultant, participant in school governance, and responsible and concerned member of the community.

Thus, the responsibility for problems in the articulation between education and work has been assigned almost exclusively to the educational sector. This assignment may result from the fact that these problems drew public attention when the market for college graduates changed into a buyers' market. Employers had no problem finding qualified workers. Instead, they had to grapple with financial problems associated with inflation and limited economic growth. To the extent that they took the time and effort to help the educational system in its effort to prepare students for work, they served as benefactors, but there was little motivation for them to play an active role and assume some responsibility.

Since both educators and employers are involved in the training of productive workers, articulation depends on a mutual understanding of training goals and processes. Because of the heavy competition for jobs, there has been a strong tendency to formulate educational goals on the basis of perceptions of what employers want. However, what employers want may not be conveyed in the same language used in educational planning, and signals sent out from the world of work may be confusing.

Educators are beginning to talk about the development of competencies. Employers frequently still screen people on the basis of their college major. To the employer, college major indicates a number of things, including background knowledge, potential trainability in a certain area, and perhaps even intelligence. For example, there seems to be a bias in favor of engineering and physical sciences. Completion of a program in one of these fields may be taken as a demonstration of intelligence.

Employers have reported that they seek people with potential to learn (e.g., Liston, 1974; Ferrin and Arbeiter, 1975), but what they mean by potential to learn has not been communicated to the campus in more specific terms than "college grades" or "college major," partly because employers themselves do not know how this potential to learn can be measured. To a large extent, this potential may be assessed by feel, that is, the impression given by the applicant during a job interview. But it has not been spelled out.

In order for employers and educators to define human development goals in mutually understandable terms, further attention must be given to the process of competency development in the work setting as well as in the classroom and to the uses of college education for specific work functions at various career levels. Greater consideration should be given to the respective roles and goals of educators and employers and to the combinations of college education and on-the-job learning that promote effective work. In this endeavor, new and meaningful partnerships should be sought in which educators and employers work together with a common purpose: the development of competent, productive individuals who will be satisfied with their lives and with their work.

References

American Telephone & Telegraph Company. *College Achievement and Progress in Management.* Basking Ridge, NJ: Personnel Research Section, American Telephone & Telegraph Company, March, 1962.

Astin, A. W., King, M. R., Light, J. M., and Richardson, G. T. *The American Freshman: National Norms for Fall 1973.* Los Angeles: Higher Education Laboratory, University of California, 1974.

Astin, A. W., King, M. R., and Richardson, G. T. *The American Freshman: National Norms for Fall 1975.* Los Angeles: University of California; Washington: American Council on Education, 1975.

Astin, A. W. "The Impact of Dormitory Living on Students." *Educational Record,* 1973, 54 (3), 204–210.

Astin, A. W. *Four Critical Years: Effects of College on Beliefs, Attitudes, and Knowledge.* San Francisco: Jossey-Bass Inc., Publishers, 1977.

Becker, G. S. *Human Capital: A Theoretical and Empirical Analysis with Special Reference to Education.* New York: Columbia University Press, 1964.

Bisconti, A. S. *College Graduates and Their Employers—A National Study of Career Plans and Their Outcomes.* Bethlehem, PA: The CPC Foundation, 1975.

Bisconti, A. S. and Solmon, L. C. *College Education on the Job—The Graduates' Viewpoint.* Bethlehem, PA: The CPC Foundation, 1976.

Bisconti, A. S. and Solmon, L. C. *Satisfaction on the Job—The Graduates' Viewpoint.* Bethlehem, PA: The CPC Foundation, 1977.

Blackburn, Robert, Armstrong, Ellen, Conrad, Clifton, Didham, James, and McKune, Thomas. *Changing Practices in Undergraduate Education.* Berkeley, CA: Carnegie Council on Policy Studies in Higher Education, 1976.

Bowen, H. R. *Investment in Learning: The Individual and Social Value of American Higher Education.* San Francisco: Jossey-Bass Inc., Publishers, 1977.

Bowman, M. J. "From Guilds to Infant Training Industries." In Anderson, C. A. and Bowman, M. J. eds. *Education and Economic Development.* Chicago: Aldine Publishing Company, 1965, 98–129.

Chickering, Arthur W. *Commuting Versus Resident Students: Overcoming the Educational Inequities of Living Off-Campus.* San Francisco: Jossey-Bass Inc., Publishers, 1974.

Chronicle of Higher Education, The. XVI (11), May 8, 1978.

Cross, K. Patricia. *Accent on Learning.* San Francisco: Jossey-Bass Inc., Publishers, 1976a.

Cross, K. Patricia. "Beyond Education for All—Toward Education for Each." *The College Board Review,* No. 99, Spring 1976b.

Ferrin, R. I. and Arbeiter, S. *Bridging the Gap: A Study of Education-Work Linkages.* Princeton, NJ: College Entrance Examination Board, 1975.

French, W. *The Personnel Management Process: Human Resources Administration and Development.* Fourth Edition. Boston: Houghton Mifflin, 1978.

Gaudet, F. J. and Carli, A. R. "Why Executives Fail." *Personnel Psychology, 10,* Spring 1957, 7–21.

Ginzberg, E. "Toward a Theory of Occupational Choice: A Restatement." *Vocational Guidance Quarterly, 20* (3), March 1972, 169–176.

Hardin, D. "We're Into Career Education." In Magisos, J. H. ed. *Career Education: The Third Yearbook of the American Vocational Association.* Washington: American Vocational Association, 1973.

Holland, J. L. "A Theory of Vocational Choice." *Journal of Counseling Psychology,* 1959 (6), 35–44.

Holland, J. L. *The Psychology of Vocational Choice.* Waltham, MA: Blaisdell, 1966.

Holland, J. L. *Self-Directed Search.* Palo Alto, CA: Consulting Psychologists Press.

Hoyt, D. P. *The Relationship Between College Grades and Adult Achievement: A Review of the Literature.* Iowa City, IA: ACT Research Reports, No. 7, September 1965.

Huttner, L., Levy, S., Rosen, E., and Stopol, M. "Further Light on the Executive Personality." *Personnel, 36,* March–April 1959, 42–48.

Liston, R. A. *On the Job Training and Where to Get It.* New York: Julian Messner, 1974.

Mahoney, Thomas A., Jerdee, Thomas H., and Nash, Allan N. *The Identification of Management Potential—A Research Approach to Management Development.* Dubuque, IA: Brown Company, 1961.

Maley, Donald. *Cluster Concept in Vocational Education.* Chicago: American Technical Society, 1975.

Mincer, J. "On-the-job Training: Costs, Returns, and Some Implications." *Journal of Political Economy,* 1962, 70, Supplement, 50–79.

Newman, F. Untitled address at the College Placement Council National Meeting, Washington, May 1975.

Ochsner, N. L. and Solmon, L. C. *College Education and Employment—The Recent Graduates.* Bethlehem, PA: The CPC Foundation, 1979.

Pace, C. R. *The Demise of Diversity.* Berkeley, CA: Carnegie Commission on Higher Education, 1974.

Parsons, F. *Choosing a Vocation.* Boston: Houghton Mifflin, 1909.

Rosen, S. "Measuring the Obsolescence of Knowledge." In Juster, F. T. ed. *Education, Income and Human Behavior.* New York: McGraw-Hill, 1975.

Rutan, P. M. and Wilson, J. T. *Career Education and English.* Boston: Houghton Mifflin, 1975.

Solmon, L. C., Bisconti, A. S., and Ochsner, N. L. *College as a Training Ground for Jobs.* New York: Praeger Publishers, 1977.

Stockford, Lee. "A Controlled Testing Program Pays Off." In Dooher, M. Joseph and Marting, Elizabeth, eds. *Selection of Management Personnel.* New York: American Management Association, 1957 (1), 138–144.

Toombs, W. Untitled address at the Middle Atlantic Placement Association, Fall Meeting, Pocono Manor, PA, October 1974.

U.S. Office of Education. *Earned Degrees Conferred.* Washington: Government Printing Office, 1976.

U.S. Department of Labor. *Dictionary of Occupational Titles.* Washington: U.S. Department of Labor, 1977.

Weisbrod, B. A. "Education and Investment in Human Capital." *Journal of Political Economy,* 1962, 70 (5), Supplement, 106–123.

Appendix

Major Area of Study, by Current Occupation

(In percentages)

Area of Major	All Occupations	Engineer	Scientist	Computer Specialist	Research/Technology Manager	Office Work: Manager or Analyst	Personnel Officer	Accountant	Marketing Specialist	Financial Specialist
Graduates of Mid-Sixties										
Number of respondents in occupation	256	33	17	20	44	32	41	27	27	15
Percent who majored in:										
Humanities, social sciences, education	26	0	6	31	2	38	61	0	48	47
Economics	5	0	0	0	11	3	5	4	0	20
Natural sciences, mathematics	17	9	94	53	18	6	5	0	0	7
Engineering	26	88	0	5	64	9	0	0	19	0
Business, accounting	27	3	0	11	5	44	27	96	33	27
Other	0	0	0	0	0	0	2	0	0	0
Graduates of Mid-Seventies										
Number of respondents in occupation	250[a]	65	14	18	15	33	19	31	30	25
Percent who majored in:										
Humanities, social sciences, education	22	2	0	12	7	42	47	0	28	52
Economics	6	0	0	0	0	12	5	3	21	12
Natural sciences, mathematics	15	9	100	59	0	6	0	7	13	8
Engineering	28	88	0	0	80	0	0	0	10	4
Business, accounting	26	2	0	24	7	40	47	87	24	24
Other	2	0	0	6	7	0	0	3	3	0

[a] Eighteen of the mid-Seventies graduates were employed in occupations classified as "Other." Of these, 78 percent majored in humanities, social sciences, or education; 11 percent in business or accounting; 6 percent in engineering; and 6 percent in one of a miscellaneous group of fields classified as "Other."

TABLE A-2 ───

Respondents Who Rated Aspects of College Education as Contributing Very Much or Moderately to Overall Job Performance, by Current Occupation

(In percentages)

Occupation	Facts or Content of Primary Study Area	General Concepts of Primary Study Area	Methods or Procedures of Primary Study Area	General Learning in College	The Study; Experience (Process of Doing Assignments)
Graduates of Mid-Sixties					
Engineer	73	82	75	67	73
Scientist	88	100	94	82	59
Computer specialist	37	58	42	63	79
Research/technology manager	54	82	72	84	82
Office work: manager or analyst	38	66	72	75	75
Personnel officer	49	68	54	71	78
Accountant	78	78	56	59	52
Marketing specialist	52	56	59	70	70
Financial specialist	47	73	50	80	80
Graduates of Mid-Seventies					
Engineer	85	91	82	71	68
Scientist	86	86	86	57	50
Computer specialist	61	89	61	78	78
Research/technology manager	64	93	79	57	79
Office work: manager or analyst	47	72	72	72	78
Personnel officer	68	68	73	90	84
Accountant	90	87	77	74	74
Marketing specialist	50	67	60	67	73
Financial specialist	28	52	60	64	84

TABLE A-3

Respondents Who Recommended Particular Study Areas, by Current Occupation

(In percentages)

Study Area	Engineer		Scientist		Computer Specialists		Research/Technology Manager		Office Work: Manager/Analyst		Personnel Officer		Accountant		Marketing Specialist		Financial Specialist	
	Mid-60s Grads (N=33)	Mid-70s Grads (N=65)	Mid-60s Grads (N=17)	Mid-70s Grads (N=14)	Mid-60s Grads (N=20)	Mid-70s Grads (N=18)	Mid-60s Grads (N=44)	Mid-70s Grads (N=15)	Mid-60s Grads (N=32)	Mid-70s Grads (N=33)	Mid-60s Grads (N=41)	Mid-70s Grads (N=19)	Mid-60s Grads (N=27)	Mid-70s Grads (N=31)	Mid-60s Grads (N=27)	Mid-70s Grads (N=30)	Mid-60s Grads (N=15)	Mid-70s Grads (N=25)
English	70	72	65	50	63	39	82	60	81	67	89	63	74	68	74	69	93	68
Languages	12	5	18	29	5	0	2	7	9	6	12	11	7	6	22	24	0	4
Other arts & humanities	15	15	6	0	11	11	32	7	22	21	22	11	15	16	33	45	20	12
Economics	70	51	24	21	16	22	84	60	72	64	61	53	78	74	81	55	93	48
Sociology	24	12	12	14	5	11	30	33	31	33	46	32	30	10	22	35	13	20
Psychology	58	35	30	21	21	45	59	60	56	58	76	74	52	42	59	59	33	44
History	9	3	0	0	0	0	8	0	19	15	17	16	7	0	19	14	13	8
Other social sciences	6	17	6	7	0	17	14	0	22	14	29	15	15	21	33	20	0	20
Biological sciences	0	6	71	79	11	0	5	0	0	6	0	0	0	3	4	0	7	8
Mathematics	82	88	100	86	84	83	68	73	50	64	29	58	59	52	52	55	73	44
Chemistry	49	60	94	93	11	6	57	13	6	9	0	5	0	3	11	7	0	0
Physics	67	68	53	79	21	17	52	3	9	5	0	5	4	7	7	10	0	0
Other physical sciences	25	18	18	14	11	6	11	0	6	11	2	0	4	0	7	0	0	0
Accounting	21	14	12	7	42	33	59	47	69	64	44	53	100	100	56	55	53	60
Business administration	61	46	29	14	42	50	86	80	84	64	93	95	89	84	89	76	67	60
Other business	21	9	12	7	11	44	34	20	50	55	56	57	59	74	59	52	47	56
Education	3	3	0	0	0	6	9	7	9	12	7	0	11	0	4	0	0	8
Engineering	97	99	6	29	32	22	77	87	19	12	2	32	7	3	19	21	13	0

TABLE A-4

Respondents Who Indicated Particular Study Areas Among Top Three Recommended, by Current Occupation

(In percentages)

Study Area	Engineer Mid-60s Grads (N=33)	Engineer Mid-70s Grads (N=65)	Scientist Mid-60s Grads (N=17)	Scientist Mid-70s Grads (N=14)	Computer Specialist Mid-60s Grads (N=20)	Computer Specialist Mid-70s Grads (N=18)	Research/Technology Manager Mid-60s Grads (N=44)	Research/Technology Manager Mid-70s Grads (N=15)	Office Work: Manager/Analyst Mid-60s Grads (N=32)	Office Work: Manager/Analyst Mid-70s Grads (N=33)	Personnel Officer Mid-60s Grads (N=41)	Personnel Officer Mid-70s Grads (N=19)	Accountant Mid-60s Grads (N=27)	Accountant Mid-70s Grads (N=31)	Marketing Specialist Mid-60s Grads (N=27)	Marketing Specialist Mid-70s Grads (N=30)	Financial Specialist Mid-60s Grads (N=15)	Financial Specialist Mid-70s Grads (N=25)
English	38	34	35	14	35	11	43	33	53	50	70	28	41	37	52	50	50	63
Languages	3	0	6	0	0	0	0	7	0	0	0	12	0	3	7	3	0	0
Other arts & humanities	3	6	0	0	15	6	2	0	6	3	5	0	7	3	15	17	0	0
Economics	16	17	6	7	0	6	16	27	25	26	13	12	33	23	33	17	57	33
Sociology	6	3	0	0	0	0	7	20	19	15	20	6	4	3	0	7	0	8
Psychology	22	12	6	7	5	22	23	27	25	33	38	35	15	10	22	27	14	21
History	0	0	0	0	0	0	5	0	10	0	8	0	0	0	4	0	0	4
Other social sciences	3	2	0	0	0	6	0	0	0	0	5	6	0	0	7	7	0	8
Biological sciences	0	0	59	50	0	0	0	0	0	0	0	0	0	0	0	0	0	4
Mathematics	38	52	59	64	60	72	21	20	10	34	10	35	15	17	7	20	50	29
Chemistry	3	25	77	86	0	0	14	7	0	6	0	0	0	3	4	0	0	0
Physics	16	22	29	14	0	11	9	7	7	0	0	6	0	3	0	0	0	0
Other physical sciences	0	0	6	14	5	0		0	3	0	0	0	0	0	0	0	0	0
Accounting	0	5	0	0	15	6	16	20	35	24	8	6	96	97	33	17	43	17
Business administration	31	15	12	7	35	56	57	40	54	57	73	94	56	40	56	43	50	54
Other business	3	0	0	0	5	11	9	7	22	15	33	35	15	33	30	13	14	21
Education	6	0	0	0	0	0	0	7	6	3	8	0	7	0	0	0	0	0
Engineering	94	97	0	21	15	11	57	74	16	6	3	12	0	3	4	17	0	4